AGRIPPINA THE YOUNGER

poems

DIANA ARTERIAN

Curbstone Books / Northwestern University Press
Evanston, Illinois

Curbstone Books
Northwestern University Press
www.nupress.northwestern.edu

Copyright © 2025 by Diana Arterian. Published 2025 by Curbstone Books / Northwestern University Press. All rights reserved.

Printed in the United States of America

10 9 8 7 6 5 4 3 2 1

Library of Congress Cataloging-in-Publication Data

Names: Arterian, Diana, author.
Title: Agrippina the Younger : poems / Diana Arterian.
Description: Evanston, Illinois : Curbstone Books/Northwestern University Press, 2025.
Identifiers: LCCN 2025002433 | ISBN 9780810148413 (paperback) | ISBN 9780810148420 (ebook)
Subjects: LCSH: Agrippina, Minor, 15–59—Poetry. | LCGFT: Biographical poetry. | Historical poetry.
Classification: LCC PS3601.R7623 A74 2025 | DDC 811/.6—dc23/eng/20250211
LC record available at https://lccn.loc.gov/2025002433

For those who look

And for my mother—memoriā et vivā et aeternā

History is a kind of study.

—SOLMAZ SHARIF

I am not inventing marvels. What I have told, and shall tell, is the truth. Older men heard and recorded it.

—TACITUS

CONTENTS

Family Tree	xii
Agrippina the Younger	3
The Rhine	4
The Palatine Hill	5

▽

Agrippina Becomes the First Noblewoman to Give Birth on Campaign...	9
The Palatine Hill	10
Germanicus's Recovering Two of Three Golden Eagle Standards	12
The Tiber	14
Agrippina, Age Three	16
The Via Sacra	17
Agrippina, Age Five	18
The Mausoleum of Augustus	19
The Death of Germanicus and the Early Message of Its Approach	20
The Mausoleum of Augustus	22
The Cremation of Germanicus	24
The Lupercal	25
The House of Livia	27
Agrippina After Her Mother Tells Her Emperor Tiberius Is Giving Her Over to Marriage	28
The Palatine Hippodrome	29
Agrippina, Age Thirteen	30
After Agrippina's Wedding to Domitius...	31
The House of Livia	32
The Death of Livia, Empress-Mother	34
The Island of Capri	35

The Exile of Agrippina's Mother by Emperor Tiberius for Four Years ...	37
Agrippina's First Pregnancy	38
The Forum	39
The Birth of Agrippina's Son, / Future Emperor Nero	40

▽

The Imperial Transition from Tiberius to Caligula	43
My Theory for Caligula's Change	44
If Caligula Had Incestuous Desire ...	46
The Funeral of Drusilla ...	47
The Island of Pandateria, Now Ventotene	49
Caligula's Changing	51
Caligula Starts with the Forced Suicide of His Adopted Son ...	53
The Island of Pandateria, Now Ventotene ...	54
The Assassination of Emperor Caligula	56
The Cryptoporticus—Palatine Hill	57
Passienus	58
When Empress Messalina Potentially Decides the Son of Agrippina ...	59
The Attempted Assassination of Agrippina's Son During Sleep	61
The Vatican Museum	62
Agrippina the Younger's Marriage to Emperor Claudius ...	64
Agrippina the Younger / Once with Power ...	65
The Material / Marital / Benefits / For Empress Agrippina	66
The Forum	67
The Celtic Chieftain Caratacus Captured ...	68

▽

The Augustan Sanctuary and Residential Complex	71
Future Emperor Nero Assumes the Toga Virilis ...	73
The Colosseum	74

The Death of Emperor Claudius at Age Sixty-Three . . .	75
The Brief Period of Agrippina Holding Total Power Through Her Emperor-Son	76
The Island of Capri	77
The First Assassination Attempt on Agrippina by Her Son, Emperor Nero	79
The Second Assassination Attempt on Agrippina by Her Son, Emperor Nero	80
During the Assassination Attempt on Agrippina in Which Her Maid, Acerronia, Tries to Survive	82
The Assassination of Agrippina	83
Emperor Nero After the Assassination of His Mother, Agrippina	84
The Bay of Baiae	86
The Uprising of Over 200,000 Tribespeople . . .	87
The Great Fire of Rome	89
Nero's Domus Aurea	90
The Death of Emperor Nero	92
The Mausoleum of Augustus	94
Elsewhere	95
Addendum—Livilla's Urn	96
Notes	105
Acknowledgments	121
Credits	123

The Julian-Claudian Family Tree

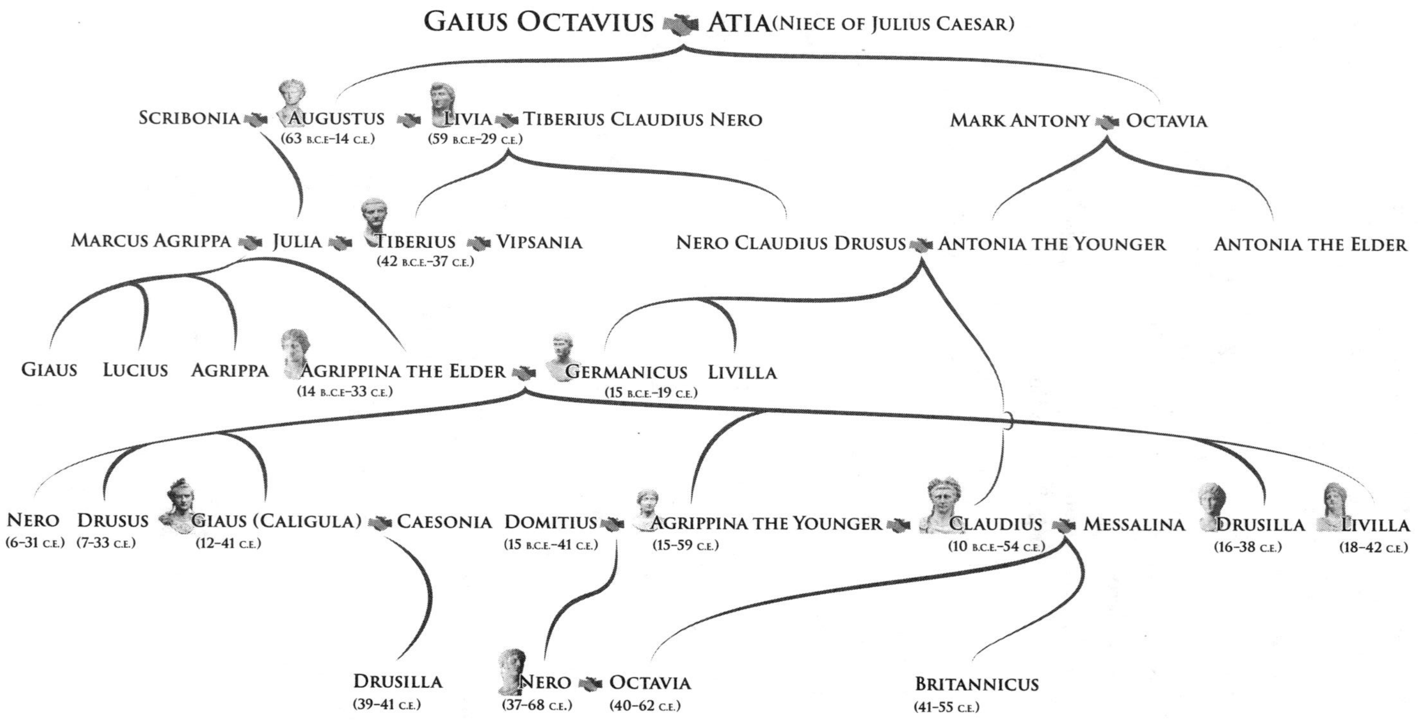

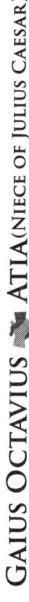

… AGRIPPINA THE YOUNGER

Agrippina the Younger

Nero had her cut down
the middle to see
the womb that formed him
And as he peered in the cleft,
that exposed organ
began to petal outward
growing and deepening
to an enormous vagina—
until he looked in
and saw only darkness
So he burned prisoners
in his garden for light
and shut her up
behind a large carving
Her remnants quietly
broke off, moving into Nero,
Piso, Vindex, Galba
So there were hauntings
and blood and exile and suicide
Nero shucked sea urchins
plucked songs on his lyre
And she continued to grow
until she held all of Rome,
which burned and was rebuilt
while she tessellated, fanned
And Agrippina smiled
with her mouth of bloody eyeteeth

The Rhine

(200 million B.C.E. *onward)*

Vast plates shifted   littler ones
with constant sounds and heat terrible
Then there was a crack   and so a river

draining new mountains   It courses in my mind
through the Ice Age   moving while loess settles
The melt raises waters   River   meandering   reworks

its Ice Age braid plain   Watch the humans from above
like small matchsticks   mine it for peat   salt   pull its salmon
ride it laden with stuffs   Watch as they claim swaths   build

crossings   develop thickly along its shores   wage wars
These dramas of land have happened everywhere   Eventually
she will be born here   That is the only reason   I care at all

The Palatine Hill

I walk the Palatine Hill for some hours, the sun beginning to heat. Then move to a bench under a large umbrella pine, brown dull needles snapping. I try to see what Agrippina saw, smell the needles. Hear beetles or crickets sounding, like rock carving into rock—or into reeds, wood. The trees perhaps different tree types, the birds, maybe. But the paths the same, the stones, the hotness.

A woman close by carries a long thin banner of wilted fabric. Walking backward, she calls information to those who follow: *Agrippina the Younger became the empress of Rome after tricking her uncle into marrying her and adopting her son. She murdered her uncle later.* And I smile, for how strange that a handful of men defined this woman's life narrative, and it continues even as the buildings she moved through have begun to crumble back to the earth.

What can History possibly say?
—ROBIN COSTE LEWIS

Agrippina Becomes the First Noblewoman to Give Birth on Campaign Becomes the Elder in an Isolated Place Later Named After the Baby Future Empress Agrippina the Younger

(15 c.e., *Oppidum Ubiorum*)

Here is the Rhine I care about   Agrippina's sons sent
to the fen's Ubii tribe   They bring two women—
midwives? healers? I don't know   The women spread

oil on Agrippina's belly to begin   One coats a finger
massages her cervix open to the size of an egg
I see it   a lens   an eye   a mouth

One woman hoists Agrippina onto her lap
while the other sets vulture feathers at her feet
This is how the poor do this   so likely here too

One woman crouches at two sets of knees and the boys
at either side press on their mother's belly   Her pain coil
twists   for hours   five bodies to bring in another

until the baby finally falls   Knowing hands
cut the cord by potsherd then pass the crier
to her brothers   The woman calls while easing out

the placenta to wash the baby with the oil   warm
Rhine water   Probably not though   unless the boys
knew the Ubii language   or the women Latin   But I like

to hear it   See the boys wipe at blood streaks and whiteness
Marvel at the pinking blue skin   her little hairs   Think
that she hummed with an importance   even then

The Palatine Hill

I am here to collapse the disk of time, stand beside her. But these aren't even all her same structures. I look at one and my mind turns to how she might have passed through an archway, hand grazing a wall. Then the placard—two hundred years after her death. It all looks ancient to my ignorant eye. And what holds or fails is so arbitrary. Frescoes from two millennia ago appear fresh. A large, relatively young marble building reduced to nubs in dirt with a dark sign as a marker. Then there was the taking of stones from one thing for another, the huge bronze statue thrashed to pieces for valuable reuse. The many sackings of Rome brought fire and blood but, amazingly, razed little.

I learn what survives best is buried. What is buried continues to surface. With each dig for a subway line, more. After excavation, a little metal gate at its lip so you can peer. Cats are quick to move in. This city built, torn, built over, so every scene is thoroughly changed since her lifetime. I can never see her visions—a strange wanting. This is a continual dance of nearly but not, sapping me.

¤

It is so hot and dusty here the moment I return to my rented space I fling my shoes and lather from my feet up to my knees. Prone on the couch under cool air, I think of the ancient cave found in France, the rock where cavepeople stubbed out torches. The carbon is dark as if just done, not thirty thousand years ago. Then the engraving found in a cave in South Africa dated over twice that old. I think, as a white American especially, this amount of time passed is beyond what I have been trained to hold in my head.

To get to old human-made structures where I grew up, you must drive through hours of desert, scramble down dirt paths into canyons. And I have done this, seen ancient Indigenous people's homes under cliffs, their hieroglyphs bigger than me. Most are riddled with bullet holes. As a child I found a flat place with countless arrowheads glinting. I held some, seeing the chips in glassy rock by hands so long ago, and I left them behind, as is respectful.

The oldest object I have ever touched that isn't a land formation was when I somehow went on a paleontological dig in New Mexico as a twelve-year-old, everyone else scientists and intrigued nonscientist adults. One paleontologist guided us in the more hardscrabble fossil finding. We hunkered down on a small mound of thumb-sized rocks. He lifted one, explained it was fossil and what to look for, how to try to find the broken piece. I scanned and picked one, holding it out *Like this?* And he took it, reuniting the nob with the other in his hand. It fit so perfectly with his surprise at my quickness he only managed *Yup.* A few days later I held a brow horn brought out from the dirt.

Germanicus's Recovering Two of Three Golden Eagle Standards

(15–17 c.e., Teutoburg Forest and Rome)

They returned to the wood of loss
Bones jut from mounds   skulls fixed

to trees   horse parts large in mud and air
charred Roman men on moldering altars

Germanicus and his soldiers spend days burying
the pieces—then deal death   shackle enemies

until two golden eagle standards are in hand
Yet the tribesmen mostly blend with trees

evanesce into the brush   slink full defeat
One aquila is never found   Emperor Tiberius

calls the soldiers home for parade
Men crowned with braided bay laurel

bear gold necklets   Breastplates
hang from them for their kills

They sing of the events   of Germanicus
He in his triumphal chariot   his robe

purple pulled across and its gold threaded
through   His face daubed red   His palms

raise   the two gold aquilae eagles   their open wings
wink in the light   Wife Agrippina and the five

small children beside   their lives
opening as the wings in the royal lines

loyalty beauty love the power possible
in the children and it is a certain glory to all

who see them   Little Agrippina not yet two beside those
in chains including the chieftain's wife and toddler boy

This is important as it was a point of pride that the Roman legions never lost their aquilae, that they never retreated. These legions's numbers were never used again, the Germanic tribal people east of the Rhine avoided after this encounter. This recovery effort brought Agrippina's father Germanicus undeniable fame, made him an heir apparent to Emperor Tiberius, who ostensibly drew him away from dangerous martial encounters afterward for this very reason.

The Tiber

They called it the Blond (Flavus) for its yellowness. Now a more green between sickly and verdant, a color glowing underneath. Where they say Romulus and Remus, abandoned, washed up under a fig tree for the lupa's finding. How Rome got its grains and goods by boat. Where bodies were often chucked. Emperor Tiberius executed with particularity—he ordered corpses left at the Gemonian Stairs, the Stairs of Mourning. Scavenger animals worried the dead for days until, eventually, soldiers pulled the bodies into the Blond. Those found guilty of treason were dragged into the Tiber on hooks, dragged through Rome *as many as twenty being so treated in a single day, including women and children.* There were corpse piles. One could not burn or bury anyone. No mourning or lingering. Tiberius's teacher once called him *mud kneaded with blood.* Sometimes, after being tried and enduring subsequent punishment, *those who wished to die were forced to live.* But how much can I trust it? Suetonius also says Tiberius *had the power of seeing even at night.*

One modern historian states, *The sources need to be seen as texts that have a clear agenda.* I encounter again and again the fraught reality of writing based on these biased texts. The modern historians who take great pains to undercut the veracity of the Roman annals but then quote them continually. Which are the grains of truth among the enormous field of wheat that shakes before me, that taunts? How to see history, not from a text, but what it writes around—a vibrating cipher?

¤

The edges of the river pushed up meters at times. Its silting was famous. The Tiber choked ports, filled and covered buildings. It surrounds one of the world's oldest Jewish ghettos, an island undesirable for its being victim to flood. The river is now contained by stone embankments, and the island a gem of the city. Some homes passed down through families for centuries. I love the thumb in the eye of their oppressors, despite the time it took. I stay at one of the Tiber's edges, a point where it's a meandering switchback. I walk along its sides, cross bridges as old as from then. The city's snaking backbone—it is my guide.

There I see a boat upturned and lodged near a bank's edge. It looks like a rusty bone in the green. Like a thing formed in nature, plucked, with lines from the water circling in yellow. Small collapsings in the body here and there, pressed in. Not so large looking until you see a crumbled chair rooted small there, gulls hunched on rock (fallen marble ruin?). Then clearly large as a whale or submarine part surfacing. Farther down, ropes tether to I don't know what, cinched together in raggedy loops. The water still, reflecting the rope lines—a light murky mirror. In darkness, rows of streetlights yellow and white, like long, brilliant torches, press downward.

Agrippina, Age Three

(*18 c.e., Anatolia*)

I reach out while in a wood
akin to hers then   nudge

a small brown thing
It might be shit save

for its ridges   papery feel
dewiness   I see a hole

in the cocoon where
whatever was pecked out

I see it   her find   in the cushion
of her palms   Little brown

ticking up with each heartbeat
Nothing   She carries it around

sets it in a sunny patch
plinks it in a wine cup

drops it in infant Livilla's bed
knots blankets   Nothing still so

she places it on a stone
smashes it with another

The Via Sacra

She homed here once—the road of thousands of parades, funerals. After the destruction of a distant enemy, the commander stood behind four horses in a chariot, face painted red. The purple toga, its dye drawn from small shells, with gold woven throughout into shapes. Later, Nero built marble columns on the road's edges. They are gone, possibly in the walls of the Colosseum. Later still, an emperor built an arch for his dead brother who besieged Jerusalem. Small, clear carvings show a coffle of stock animals, people, all circled together with ropes. L'Arc de Triomphe in Paris copies it.

The road is laid with gray stones, each like the bottom of an elephant foot. The shapes are uneven, yet pushed neatly up into each other. What can and cannot last two thousand years is consistently beyond my grasp. The stone different stone, perhaps. Maroon wall murals in one place, yes. A whole building in another, no. So maybe the rock path is Agrippina's rock path. I tremble at the closeness, self-consciously snap a photo of my shadow on our rocks, our shadows aligned maybe. This woman of books only before, but now a blurring, for my path is her path and the bodies the same.

No marker for her home, only plaster-worn brick ruins. Some parallel and safe, others look like chalk fan sprays around the doors. Tall dark metal bars in front. But maybe this one here she walked from.

Agrippina, Age Five
(20 c.e., Antioch)

She sees the trail of gore and follows
Finds a small roe deer   arrow almost

through the neck   Crouching she
pushes it out   breaks the tip

slips the shaft from the deer as it kicks
weakly   She lifts its head to her lap

strokes between the eyes
cradles the ear with her little hand

Ticks move to the hairless arms   Blood
pumping out the hole   then less

The breaths more and more shallow
She hums as her mother does the baby

The deer's tongue slips quietly
from between its teeth   The girl still

pets as the woods and head grow cold
She eyes the large warm belly

wants to press   massage whatever
out   build a fire beneath so

the flesh will open and show
She sees the fire   the fur

all blackly twisted   skin splitting
the pink fawn's eye   on her

The Mausoleum of Augustus

Imagine a three-tiered red cake, each lower layer wider than what rests above. When built, the levels were covered with earth and bushy cypresses. The architectural procession all topped with a golden statue of Augustus, maybe. It was once buried in Tiber River silt, thought lost. A years-old article describes it as *a city-block-sized monument which has been used as a toilet by tramps since falling into disrepair and now stands moldering behind fences*. Enormous full cypresses now rise from the lowest cake layer. It sinks into the earth.

Though it's shut up for restoration, I can see around from the walkway above. The edges look mossy, but that is due to its size—full plants cling to its bleaching brick. A man in orange landscapes, takes a whipping machine to the mausoleum's side, chips off the smaller greens. Then other men unload from a white-cab truck that pulls down the ramp to a two-hundred-foot-tall archway topped with a smaller enclosed arch braced with scaffolding. They unlock the inner gate, enter, and disappear.

¤

Agrippina did the long march from the city to this place to bury her family members many times. Emperors, without fanfare, often set the urns of mothers and brothers banished by the emperor prior. Agrippina's great-grandfather and great-grandmother, grandmother and grandfather, mother and father, brothers and sisters, uncles, aunts, husbands, and stepsons were burned and placed inside—most in her presence.

Agrippina was never interred here. Nero put her in the ground, and today no one knows where. Nero himself was buried in the mausoleum of his father.

I learn the mausoleum will open after a three-year restoration. I try to find images of the interior and am surprised by its being almost fully in open air. What look like doorways to crypts spill foliage. All is exposed, save for the innermost burial chamber—a perfect circle at its center. The floor plan reveals a panopticon. Aerial views show an eye, pupil white as from a flash.

The Death of Germanicus and the Early Message of Its Approach

(20 c.e., *Antioch Epidaphne*)

Days into illness   Germanicus demands a study
of the house   In one shadowed corner   attendants

find lead tablets thin and curled shut   GERMANICUS
pushed into the soft gray with a careful hand   then a just

as careful line raked through   In another
a wizened finger   ash with the rusty look of blood

Death hovers there for days   He names it
poison   Wife Agrippina by the couch

pets damp hair as he asks   *If my enemy
is here   what can that mean for you?*

. . .

The year prior   Germanicus sails the edges
of empire   He touches shore to hear the oracle

of Apollo at Claros   The oracle asks Germanicus
only to speak his name   The oracle then leaves

for darkness of a nearby cave   Feeling for water
on hands and knees   he cups to his mouth

that which gives him sight and shortens his life
Returned to the temple   the illiterate priest

speaks in verse   head lolling
unfocused eyes   words barely heard

This is important as Germanicus was beloved, was the next emperor, it seemed—with many sons to succeed him. Tiberius likely had him poisoned, though this order wasn't proven publicly. When news reached Rome of Germanicus's death, people threw stones at temples and, one historian claims, "some flung their household gods into the street and cast out their newly born children."

The Mausoleum of Augustus

The *Res Gestae Divi Augusti* was a long funerary inscription for Emperor Augustus carved on bronze columns and rock all over, in the many languages the empire contained, for its many literate citizens to know. It is found mostly whole in Ankara, and in pieces in Rome near Augustus's urn at his mausoleum. He wrote it himself. I wonder at the process of writing your own obituary in the first person, to capture a habitually unmet legacy.

At one point, Augustus lists all the structures he built—almost two dozen, most of them temples. His *Res Gestae* also states, *Janus Quirinus, which our ancestors ordered to be closed whenever there was peace, secured by victory, throughout the whole domain of the Roman people on land and sea, and which, before my birth is recorded to have been closed but twice in all since the foundation of the city, the Senate ordered to be closed thrice while I was princeps.*

Augustus didn't care much about appearances, Suetonius explains—*He was so far from being particular about the dressing of his hair, that he would have several barbers working in a hurry . . . while at the very same time he would either be reading or writing something.* This makes him more appealing, somehow.

The mausoleum was employed as a garden by some major Roman families in the Renaissance. At the start of the 1800s, it was a circus.

¤

While now surrounded by buildings, the imperial mausoleum was then on the city's outskirts, enclosed in green. A long, thin, dusty road connected it to the Ara Pacis Augustae altar, which was in pieces for centuries. Those pieces were eventually found under a theater. Reassembled, it is a large, walled, open-air structure. Steps lead to the altar within, the relief marble edgings all curly flora, carved portraits of figures historians argue over. In the museum, you can move inside the roofless rectangle. Unwitting American, I see no rope cordoning off what is forbidden, so I sit on an altar stair to take it in as a guard swings over ordering me up, and I'm standing quickly, worrying over my lasting effect on marble despite the brief touch (I realize it is not small).

The altar shows child Germanicus holding his mother's hand. A slightly older Domitius (Nero's father) pulls a robe of someone labeled simply "Drusus," but there are many men named that so why tugging on these particular robes I don't know. Future Emperor Claudius is nowhere. Some faces point away, other figures mere tracings of unknown. Though the whole of it is reassembled, the historians's guide for identifying its carved figures is from what they have found on a few ancient coins. Is my work so different? I look closer—try to discern even a sliver.

The Cremation of Germanicus

(20 c.e., *Antioch*)

The body is on display for days to prove
murder   Dark spots show on the skin

white froth caked at the mouth's edges
Widow Agrippina and her small children

watch the loved body burn   then the slow
shoveling of ash   They listen to bones

clink against his stone urn held
at her chest for the days's ride over hard

wintry seas   The heart was found whole
in the bones   as a poisoned one is

The Lupercal

Several meters below Palatine ground is a dome stuck with shells and tile. It is found by accident, as with so many things. Afraid to dig in the dome for fear of causing collapse, archaeologists push a camera through a dusty hole, scan the space, and claim to have found the Lupercal—the cave place where the she-wolf didn't kill the the twins Romulus and Remus who will try to kill each other. She stands looking outward as if for danger as the two boys are below, her milk in bands down their throats. The grotto is part dirt and there is excitement at that. Its truth of this being a cave, the nursing here, then later Roman veneration with mosaics pressed into mortar within. The wolf saved them from death only to have one start one of the largest empires of history with his brother's blood.

For killing of close kin in ancient Rome, you were beaten with rods, sewn into a large leather sack with a dog, rooster, monkey, and snake, and thrown into a sea or river.

The Latin "lupa" is also a term for sex worker. *Could it be that a local whore rather than a local wild beast had found and tended the twins?* one modern historian asks. The fig tree at the edge of the Tiber where they washed up was apparently replanted in the Forum.

Horace writes, *A bitter fate pursues the Romans / and the crime of a brother's murder, / ever since blameless Remus's blood was spilt onto the ground, / to be a curse.*

¤

The image of them below the wolf and her looking out and protective, teeth sharp and sure, is the city's icon—more prevalent than the pope even. The milky stripes. But the wolf portion of the sculpture predates the suckling twins. A sculptor added them later, which makes it even more Roman to me—the building upon the ancient for meaning.

I imagine Agrippina, small, finding the space by chance in the darkness and whistling to hear the height, fingers in the small seashells, tiles, everywhere in the windless place, a bright eagle at the dome's center.

I ask an archaeologist guide offhand about the discovery and she says, *No, it's just a fountain.*

The House of Livia

I spend the morning looking for its door, walk circles over the Palatine Hill. The bricks winnow. It takes me three days to find out how to gain entry after hours of pacing—only when I ask the right person, who explains you need special tickets. So I make what I worry is an expensive phone call required to get them. Days later, a small group of us includes three American women in Rome for Mother Teresa's canonization (which I sleep through, mere blocks away, but see the ground peppered with petals and paper strips the rest of the week). One woman sees my little flip notebook and asks if I'm a reporter. I want to open up and tell her everything, Agrippina and poetry, but just say, *No, no.*

An anthropology graduate student leads us inside the blessedly cold underground. Agrippina's home, once, with her great-grandmother.

¤

Livia features heavily in the novel *I, Claudius*. Reading it, I was bored. I skimmed. The author mainly took from what other men had written, and I had read them. *So much research—was it worth it?* I thought ruefully. Then, *God, am I doing the same thing?* Left to my own devices, perhaps I had.

Rankled by the novel, I dreaded watching the more-famous miniseries. The characters were monotonous, immutable even as life lobbed enormous changes at them, as they aged. But Siân Phillips's Livia was incredible. Odd, gorgeous, arresting. *Because I was a woman, you pushed me into the background,* she tells Augustus's body she has poisoned into a corpse. Stately tears make their way with her words. As I watched her, I thought, *This woman deserves every award she ever got.*

But—*Agrippina only at the end???* I scribbled during an episode near the series's completion. *Ugh. Good riddance.*

Agrippina After Her Mother Tells Her Emperor Tiberius Is Giving Her Over to Marriage

(28 c.e., Palatine Hill, Rome)

She goes up to the curved-roof Temple
of Cybele alone   The throned goddess
all smooth marble save for her face—
black meteorite   The celestial fleck

shot down to Anatolia brought from the coast
to Rome by a single line   of women
Thousands passed the raw rock with care
carved to features upon its arrival   I want to sit

in the goddess's stone lap   think Agrippina
would want this but likely not   It is I who rages
wishes to scratch at the meteorite's little holes
Though this union is the requirement for her power

what leads to the day when Agrippina herself will be carved
life-sized in basanite   That black stone is almost as precious
as Cybele's pitted face   Basanite is nearly impossible
to shape—a sculptor's special torture

This is important as Emperor Tiberius chose Agrippina's husband for her, a praetor named Domitius Ahenobarbus over thirty years her senior. Agrippina was maybe thirteen. This was not an uncommon age for a bride. Domitius was roundly hated, apparently hit a child in the road with his carriage as the boy was playing. Even if untrue, the story tells of a general feeling.

The Palatine Hippodrome

Not a space to move horses around as the Greeks did—here, slow strolls in loops by the important families homed in a ring around the place. Walls raised to shade the grassy walkway, its shape like a long pill. Semicircular fountains of marble to sit and feel coolness coming off water.

A huge exedra clings to a wall's side above the oval of green. In a diagram, it looks like a building cut lengthwise with its dome columns—a halved mushroom cap all marble-white. Now, like a large thing bombed. Tufts of light tall grass spring from its jagged edges. Black streaks from water move down like hairy vines.

She must have walked around here, surely. As a child, at the very least, but probably after.

What was all white once is now down to a bleached red. Farther below, the fine careful brick chipped back like bark. Beneath, rougher rock mortared in place. One Corinthian column top, leaves pushing into loops, is lopped off and juts out from the dirt, like a kind of bench. A clutch of smoothed bright stone columns is arranged on their sides in a neat line, cracked into parts. Put there, they look like bodies laid out in the grass. Other large columns all rubbed away down to brick nubs, ringed with light marble at their bases.

A thin white rope cordons off the center of the oval, which contains work of contemporary artists. One is metallic silver letters as large as me stuck into weighted stands in a semicircle that spell LOSER. (Perhaps this is the side where Remus died from Romulus's hand.) A woman stands in front of it while her companion snaps a picture. A simple white neon sign glows HERSTORY in a covered walkway.

Agrippina, Age Thirteen
(28 c.e., Rome)

Domitius gives her a ring of iron
Agrippina fingers it under her robes
while slaves weave her hair with flowers

place gold on her neck and wrists
She thinks of the man   older
than her father ever was

At the ceremony   a pregnant sow is brought forward
dark and wreathed in leaves   Wine   crumbs
from holy cake are dusted on its brow

for the goddess Ceres   for Terra Mater
for this marriage   A man raises his axe
blunt-side-down   strikes the sow

slices the stunned animal's throat   opens
her belly   The priest pushes fetal piglets aside
handles the entrails close to his eyes

looking for flaws   Another man
places the insides on an altar for burning
Domitius watches Agrippina while the men

butcher the pig   char the guts   She does not look away
The priest steps into the blood   face covered   prays
in whispers   a flute drowning out any ominous sounds

After Agrippina's Wedding to Domitius
As with Custom
What Follows
(28 c.e., *Lavinium*)

In her hands   a torch   A long grand line
marches down the road of pale dirt—
a dark thread behind her   pulling

Domitius waits with another torch
a bowl of water   Guests feast
I can even tell you what they ate

Probably animals cooked in leeks
and wine   melon sucking into honey
Agrippina follows Domitius into a room

A slave waits in a corner   begins to undress
the bride   She slowly naked   Then on
the couch   arms at her sides   eyes up

He stares at her body   pale in the dark
hairs   just there   breasts beginning
He pinches a small nipple between thumb

and knuckle   Agrippina turns her face
toward   or away   you decide
I don't want to imagine anymore

The House of Livia

They name it hers for the IULIA AUG[USTA] stamped in the lead that funneled water into the cellar. There is a covey of us behind an archaeology student as our guide. He unlatches the low gate with a definitive *clank* and we descend through the vestibule entrance into delicious coolness. Three large open-arched rooms face us with careful purpley frescoes. What is purple was once red. This is where the empress-mother received guests. There is a tablinum with Io painted depicting her rescue from a cow's shape back into a woman's. Diana here in aniconic form of a quiver, leaning on a baetyl obelisk for Apollo. The paintings are architectural. They give depth that isn't there, pushing back into stone with color, shadow.

Dark floor tiles have a white trim arranged like fish scales. And they have survived two thousand years. My feet on the tiny tiles where her tiny feet once were, when she lived here. What does my breathing here do? The sweat and movement? It must make this all destroy itself. The cost worth it to archaeologists, for our experience funds more excavation, repair.

¤

Augustus loved Livia, left a wife and had Livia leave her husband while pregnant so she could marry the emperor. Suetonius writes that Augustus *loved and esteemed her to the end and without a rival*. He had no children with Livia, yet it was something he *earnestly desired*. One contemporary pointed out that Augustus was succeeded by the son of an enemy—for the father of Tiberius was no friend of the emperor who stole his wife.

While pregnant with the Tiberius, Livia attempted to know the sex of her baby. Suetonius explains how *she took an egg from under a setting hen, and when she had warmed it in her own hand . . . a cock with a fine crest was hatched.*

Livia is thought to have murdered any who vied for her son Tiberius's seat on the emperor's throne, thought to be Agrippina's model, knowing the powers of plants on the unexpecting body, how to ply an emperor-husband—the contained rein and then terrifying gallop of an emperor-son. How a woman who had the ear of the most powerful man in Rome terrified the senators and often drove arguments for a return to the Republic—to destroy the imperial structure.

The Death of Livia, Empress-Mother
(29 C.E., Palatine Hill, Rome)

Emperor Tiberius sent for to come to kiss
his mother's mouth closed   press her eyes shut

He remains on his far island of Capri   Livia
is surrounded by grandchildren and great-grandchildren

none of whom will die   with this quiet
Her breath out and body closed up

She is set on earth as when born
cleaned and ready on a couch

a heavy coverlet up to her neck
spruce bough at the door

Slaves wash the body nightly
It a slow green   as in a damp place

Each day Agrippina sits   hand on
covered foot   until the day the body

begins to blister   flies and others nibble at
the seams   The flesh pressing out   no perfume

can snuff   A funeral   then the full Forum   All feel
the power she carved for emperor-son so coolly absent

This is important as Livia was the most powerful woman in Rome, and everyone knew it. Livia's funeral was held at the Forum, a rare honor. Her son, Emperor Tiberius, was to be the one to speak of her life—or at least that was the custom. But it is Caligula who speaks. The Roman people began to see Caligula as capable and thoughtful, a leader like his father Germanicus might have been.

The Island of Capri

It is here where, when Tiberius had a bath, he had boys ("little fishes") tickle his parts underwater. Some *unweaned babies put to his organ as though to the breast*, Suetonius tells us. When done with them, he pushed them off cliffs into churning water. Adults Tiberius found to be criminals were brought here and tortured, then *cast headlong into the sea before his eyes, while a band of marines waited below for the bodies and broke their bones with boat hooks and oars.*

I don't know about the little fishes, but the dumped bodies of "criminals" seems likely.

I don't get to Capri (time, money) and feel some pangs of regret, as it looks very beautiful. A good place for being. Where Emperor Tiberius hid for years—from wife? mother? public? Caligula was with him too for some time, for who knows what. In explanation, Tiberius apparently said of this future emperor that he was *rearing a viper for the Roman people.*

¤

In the 1979 film *Caligula*, its famous orgy scene has Emperor Tiberius and Caligula walk around a dimly-red-lit area while people have all kinds of physical fun. You don't always know what body parts are what. Many are actors who worked in porn. But there are some people there who are not participating in the orgy—twins conjoined at the head, the torso. There is a shot of arms with prosthetic extra hands, their owner's face we never see. A person with one leg crawls around.

After years of reading and research and travel, it is this scene that finally clicks an understanding into motion in my mind. When I realize the Western world's obsession—the continual return to this era, these people—for what it is: a freak show.

We watch with glee. We define ourselves as not-them. And while hardcore sex is what the film is known for, the inclusion of differently abled bodies inserts something into that scene beyond vaguely-history-themed pornography. It is the heart of our fascination made plain. One modern scholar writes, *anomalous creatures have long been displayed at fairs and circuses, extorting shudders of revulsion and delight.*

The Exile of Agrippina's Mother by Emperor Tiberius for Four Years Until She Dies Where Her Mother Died And a Daughter Will

(29–33 c.e., the island of Pandateria)

She is shipped to a speck
learns of time's new shape
of sons   How one tells his guard

give me a dagger so I may open myself up
The other swallows pinched bed stuffs
to stall starvation   Both bodies so diffuse

only through great pains were they gathered
The guards mock her *dux femina dux femina*
when they lay food down until she rises

shouts *I am Ceres made mortal of Caesar*
you cannot know me and the guard
slaps a hand over her mouth raises

the other fist down such that her eye
arcs from her face gone and that
is when she stops taking food

Agrippina's First Pregnancy

(35 C.E., *Lavinium*)

It has been months since she bled
beyond murky water   She hopes

One night she dreams
the birth   The baby

out but changing quick
Heavy like a stone   Skin

pale   hardening bark
marble cracks   peels

thin   like paper
She wakes—

a fan of blood
bright as death

The Forum

Before the heat and crowd, I see the Forum above from a street. Few full structures, though some walls, their scalloped arches. Bottoms of marble columns, or some as if shattered and glued. Others complete, the building gone. Most coin-like chunks, large, all around.

While down in the guts, I eye the Domus Tiberiana palace with several skinny looping archways. Later, I read it is where Nero stood a teenager, was named emperor before the people.

Palm-sized orange fish dart, fill a round hazy fountain, a tall marble arch pushed up inside the wall above. Greens on a teardrop shelf, enormous, slanting from the arch top. Mineral layer spreads on mineral layer, from water over millennia, into a rockish thing. The organic slope with rusty bottom edging. Water dribbles from its base, invisible. Plants cover it, some with small purple flowers, others flattening up the marble above like forced hands, leaves pressing on carved leaves.

While most structures merely have one column to serve as a marker for their existences, a basilica built over a millennium ago is startling for its still-wholeness. Its large bronze doors are a patchy green, ancient, with a lock that still clicks into security.

The Birth of Agrippina's Son, Future Emperor Nero

(37 c.e., *Antium*)

Women set Agrippina on a hard bed   raise her feet
place amulets around her   A bitch's placenta
on one thigh   snake's sloughed skin on the other

I have learned of these rituals and struggle
to not find them strange be compelled   Cloth
soaked in warm oil   spread flat across the belly

bladders filled   set on her sides   This at least
a help   Nothing but terrible pain for hours
The women begin to tire as darkness

edges in   Agrippina pales   The midwife
moves the dog placenta to Agrippina's pubis
strokes her cervix   to coax it open   The women

pull Agrippina into a chair surround her   she
barely conscious   The assistants push down
on her belly   midwife reaching to stretch the cervix

Her fingers hook tiny ankles   pull out the baby
bloody-bright in the dawn   One woman catches
the shit that comes with him   And we know this

future emperor breech only for Pliny's writing
OF PRODIGIOUS AND MONSTROUS BIRTHS   He references
Agrippina's memoir   with no direct quotation

▽

if a woman fights,
she must fight by stealth,
with invisible gear
—H.D.

The Imperial Transition from Tiberius to Caligula
(37 c.e., Rome)

When the Roman public
learns of Tiberius's death
they call for his body

to be thrown in the Tiber
When they hear Caligula
has power they cry   Our

babe Our star line the streets
for twenty miles to greet him
They drink to excess cut and burn

hundreds of thousands of livestock
Caligula abolishes treason
recalls Tiberius's many exiles

destroys treason trial papers in public
puts his sisters on the coin   brings
ashes of his mother and brothers

to the Mausoleum of Augustus
quietly sets Tiberius's urn too
among his ancestors there

The rusty tang
of animal blood still
lingers when he falls ill

This is important as Emperor Tiberius was hated and Caligula, son of the ideal Roman, Germanicus, was beloved. Romans felt they had been saved after decades of Tiberius's conscriptions, orders to pull the dead through Rome's streets on hooks, leaving body piles. Caligula was, at first, a careful emperor—a truth often glossed over. Caligula's attachment to his sisters was notable and strange, as women were legally second-class citizens.

My Theory for Caligula's Change
(37 c.e., Rome)

A slave finds him flushed
to purple   words barely coming

The physician burns sage
applies fennel suggests sacrifice

So servants cut into animals
for days   The god is unmoved

If it were a hundred years later
probably deep lancings in the young

emperor's limbs   blood darkly
pooling in plates   Here the physician

details the burring of a coin-
sized hole into the skull

After opium   hands
press him down   the drill

twists in   winding the sound
of bubbles slow behind his ear

Enough bone lifted   the wound
dressed in unwashed moorit wool

soaked in oil   kept damp with fresh
leaves spread over   And he steadies

differently   In weeks it knits shut
soon skin and hair covering   Then sister

Drusilla suffers from the fever tearing
through Rome like a fire   dies in a night

If Caligula Had Incestuous Desire Even Perhaps Action

(23 c.e., *Palatine Hill, Rome*)

I pluck the thread of Caligula fucking his sisters   pluck to follow its ends   Its start   Caligula/Little Boots for the caligulae—studded soles tooled for the child's feet   Apparently no one called him this as an adult but we do now   He padded around his father's camps   mush of mud and slicked grass   trees alongside   the feet through it   with webbed leather   A soldier maybe starts play then something more stifling   play with bolts of pain pet and hushed through   This harm cycle then   Or born with the deviance maybe   Maybe Agrippina Drusilla Livilla giggle in a ring take turns lifting robes to probe and find   Caligula seeing   Sits wanting to try   The girls quiet   look   say nothing   Perhaps the plucked thread vibrates most at the annals   Tales a painting   a jab to maim the family   What kind of emperor puts his sisters on coins   makes them vestal virgins   wails so much when one dies   when women had so little value?   *Why do that unless lust is behind it?* is the logic   Their family's potential glory undeniable—so much it pushes all to death   forced starvation   blades   starvation as protest   poisons—save for one   one spared   who all agree was Caligula's focus   love   whom he called his little wife

The Funeral of Drusilla
The One Child of Agrippina the Elder and Germanicus to Die Without Violence

(38 c.e., Rome)

For hours Caligula will not let them
take the body   until he does
Slaves wash the corpse   anoint it
with perfumes oil   dress it in fine

garments One slave plaits the hair
another places a coin on the tongue
pressed with the corpse's likeness and that
of her sisters and brother After eight nights

musicians lead a processional in the dark
blow mournful songs Hired women cry
Persons bear waxen masks of ancestors
and follow   Drusilla is borne on a couch

covered with leaves   fabric of gold   purple
carried by husband   uncle Claudius Caligula
all in browns and grays   Livilla and Agrippina
follow in white   Is this so different from what

we do? What I have seen? We often expose
less So watch   The oration Caligula
wails through Then to the burning place
Dark foliage in layers   the couch there

Her husband raises the torch up
but the emperor seizes it lights
As Drusilla burns Caligula beats
his chest   claws his cheeks

After hours   once mostly ashes
the men gather them in an urn
of carved marble   Caligula sets it
in the mausoleum with the other dead

The Island of Pandateria, Now Ventotene

A friend is passing through Rome and we get to the small volcanic island of exile. Train, train, ferry early in the morning. Its population in the hundreds, there is a museum there with mostly two-handled jugs called amphoras with bases tapering to a point for storage on ships—objects the color of bruises covered in light wormy twists dredged from the seafloor and shipwrecks. There is a woman's skeleton and some coffin bits around her, her bones woodlike. It is here I learn I cannot see where Agrippina was held, closed off from us, far from town, at the island's edge. The docent gives tours in Italian, but only after the last boat leaves that night.

I walk and find a large placard that reads *La Storia e l'Archeologia*, umber plastic on plastic with words almost lost, the parts dark as if from soot pushing deep into the edges, whole columns of words eaten. White veins thread all over, some peeling to the gray beneath.

It reads:

> *luogo di esilio per le donne delle*
> *ulia de Flavia che si opposero ai det-*
> *mpero o che me intralliarono le poli-*
> *lia (figlia liberale di Augusto),*
> *Maggiore, ivilla, Ottavia e Flavia*

Maggiore finishing *Agrippina Maggiore*—Agrippina the Elder, [L]ivilla, Octavia: imprisoned women who died here.

The veins on the placard widen through the image of a stone face—a woman's face. It could be anyone. There is even English, but it is smaller and the cracks and burn-dark edges have taken it.

It is while here Agrippina learns her husband Domitius is dead. She felt relief probably, but I'm uncertain it is relief alone, another feeling quick—her son there without her. You can't see the mainland shore from here. Agrippina probably thought she would waste for years, if not die on the island. Caligula was young, and no emperor had ever been assassinated.

¤

My friend and I move from the main courtyard up to a lovely restaurant where the owner herself serves us fish and stuffed squash blossoms and herby bread. She asks what I'm doing here, so far from home, and I tell her of my hope to see the ruins even from water. *I know a man—Rocco. He has a boat.* So we are soon out on water very blue. It's clear at the edges, then drops to dark.

Rocco flies past the ruins before I have a moment. The museum called it *a curtain of brick*. Most tumbled into sea. Below the brick, paddle leaf on yellow stone. Door-like holes high up on ledges that go nowhere, a drop from a cliff. The sky shows through the door holes like blue tombstones.

Caligula's Changing

(39 c.e., Rome)

Caligula orders a marble stable built
a manger of ivory   Gives his horse Incitatus
purple cloth blankets   a collar set with ring
upon ring of gems   feeds him oats and flakes

of gold   Has two miles of floating bridge built
grain boats for pontoons   dirt mounds leveled
like the Appian Way   all set in the Gulf of Baiae
Alexander the Great's breastplate from

the sarcophagus fastened on him   a crown
of oak leaves   a cloak of gold cloth   He rides
Incitatus back and forth at a full gallop
for days   This period you may know   when he

is played by the actor from *A Clockwork Orange*
or the other actor from *Alien* (the latter is better)
Both renditions make him even more wild
and brutal than the annals dare   In one he eats

the fetus of his child out of his sister while dressed
as Zeus   *This says more about the writer than history*
I think   The annals instead tell us of the Egyptian
obelisk set in a new vast racetrack   A boat   larger

than any other—gem-encrusted sterns   marble floors
A buoyant palace   His order for the boring through
hard flint for nothing   His baths in perfume   oils
Dissolving pearls in vinegar for drinking   He spills

gold coins to feel the metal on his soles   rolls in the piles
Money dwindles   Imports stop   He claims steed Incitatus
will be a consul   or priest   He speaks to the moon
often looks far off   bouts of staring   Then the killings start

---

This is important as Emperor Tiberius spared Caligula because one soothsayer told him Caligula "had no more chance of becoming emperor than of riding about over the Gulf of Baiae with horses." Caligula eventually tips into mania, a paranoia so deep he will exile his own sisters, to whom he had given unprecedented honors. After almost a quarter of a century under Tiberius, the Romans had thought Caligula would be their savior.

Caligula Starts with the Forced Suicide of His Adopted Son With Whom He Was Named to Share Power

(39 c.e., Rome)

His tongue moves
for death   It kills

senators   father- and brother-
in-law   Uncle Claudius

spared thought a fool all
stutter   idiot walking drags

a leg behind   After meals
Claudius asleep until pelted

with olive pits   shoes
slipped on his hands

. . .

Caligula fucks someone
who produces letters of a plot

He thinks sisters Agrippina Livilla
Drusilla's widower all scheming

Soldiers kill his brother-in-law
sisters sent to the Pontine Islands

Caligula confiscates their things
and there is so much

the wagons clog the streets
interrupt city supplies

The Island of Pandateria, Now Ventotene

Agrippina and sister Livilla bring sponges up to the rock veins, sandy brown, worn, black sea urchins. Dead Queen Anne's lace and garlic scapes stiffen up the brick. Cliffs tumble into water, black volcanic rock. Small grottoes, protuberances against blue. A volcanic layer as if moving outward. And water, water pushed into being.

My friend and I strip to underwear and dive in once the boat driver Rocco finds a quiet niche. And he follows, a body of intuition in the sea. Warm saltwater stings the lips. Delicate striped fish peck fuzzy rocks. I flatten on my back, waves moving over, ears hit with the snap of waves. Underneath, thousands of alpheid shrimp clack their claws, the sound of fire.

Was her hair in a tight braid? Salt in the roots, pinching frost of salt off the eyebrows for days. What did they swim in? Made to harvest sponges, for what?

The warm upper band and cooler low where she felt along, a coarse but full give.

Prickly pear spilling from—clinging to—the cliff edges or land.

¤

The closest island as you can see on this clear day bears a large stone structure. It looks white in the sun against the blue. A relatively recent prison, built by Italian rulers in 1795.

The museum here shows the building plan—a literal panopticon. While the ancient Roman prison-villa of Pandateria crashed into water, its stones taken for homes, almost two millennia later Mussolini brought more prisoners to the same sea, on another shelf of land nearby.

How a place can alter and cycle back, crumble, then be reused, its function revived for its isolation. Pandateria and others are a model. As in Jeremy Bentham's panopticon prison—*Each Cell is an island: the inhabitants, shipwrecked mariners cast ashore.*

¤

But then, years later, I find out she was never there, never at all. She was on some other spit of dirt nearby: Tyrrhenia (now Ponza). She didn't even have her sister for company. Or maybe they were both on Tyrrhenia. Everyone has the same names, is sent to the same archipelago. Books are vague. Websites confuse translations. I read and read but can't know for sure.

The Assassination of Emperor Caligula

(41 c.e., Rome)

He dresses in cloaks of jewels   tunics and bracelets
silks   soldier shoes women's shoes as Mercury

as Apollo   He carries a trident   a thunderbolt
takes up Jupiter as a name   How might a man

believe himself a god   much less several?
Money spent to nothing and so comes famine

Secret meetings while Caligula plans time in Egypt
for worship of his godly body   One night

he visits sister Drusilla's crypt alone with milk
and flowers   Then homeward   finds three

of the Praetorian Guard with blades out that move
through his exquisite fabrics   flesh over and over

to thirty wounds until blood in the fine cloth
and also his wife   One man clutches

their baby Drusilla by the feet   brings
her down against a wall   just once

The Cryptoporticus—Palatine Hill

A row of stunted arched hallways were once for storage, guards's homes. The brick edges are now worn until they poke out like little red teeth. These were long and deep, once. Cool. A small sign explains their purpose and also Caligula's assassination within a tunnel—perhaps even in this very gallery. A metal post with delicate links strung to another metal post keeps me from entering. Thinking of the dagger pushing in and the muscle clenching as it does for protection from bleeding, yet works for the blade, tearing more.

Caligula ordered executions by a thousand cuts at times, days long, parents of the doomed there and made to watch. And Caligula there too, saying, *Strike so that he may feel that he is dying.* Who did the cuts, I wonder? What was their thought? Desperation? Glee? Boredom?

At a dinner near two consuls, the emperor begins to laugh. One consul asks the emperor for the humor. *What do you suppose, except that a single nod and both of you could have your throats cut on the spot?* Caligula claimed victory over the sea after sending soldiers to the English Channel. With no enemy there, he demanded shore shells for booty and displayed the shard spoils of Neptune upon their return. He sacrificed flamingos and peacocks.

Maybe this is all possible. I believe the bird sacrifice tidbit more than anything else.

Caligula was the first emperor ever assassinated (Julius Caesar was a dictator). His spirit was seen moving at the Palatine Hill for months after his death and hasty burial—until Agrippina moved his ashes to the Mausoleum of Augustus with her other family members' ashes.

Soot brushes the ceiling of one of the archways. Archaeological objects of various rectangles are shrouded in white canvas below, white-and-red-checked twine holding on in loops. A fern sprays green from a red wall. What looks like golden straw flecks the ground.

Passienus

(41 c.e.)

I want to write Agrippina happy. Bring her home from an exile she thought would take her life. Reunite her with her son. Give her the quiet good of her marriage after stark circumstances on an island. Passienus was known for his wit and laugh. I think him kind. He had been previously married to Agrippina's sister-in-law, Domitia. I imagine a moment, years prior: Domitia grabs Agrippina's braid to pull her close, slaps her face, and Agrippina makes a vow in her mind. What is known is Domitia hated her, was generally venomous. Passienus leaves this woman for Agrippina. Their marriage a vengeance mingled with goodness. Their fucking a glory. I think of it as the first golden age of her adult life. Sweet years of care, Passienus playing with the boy. Holding him up in a field in the air, the flash, laughing, and Agrippina's coin-bright eyes on them. Joy she had only known, otherwise, in the love between her parents. A thick calm. Maybe an old feeling tugged over her, novel for its distance since childhood: real security. Maybe another feeling began to peck at the good, less alien: desiring more than this life.

I don't know. And I don't know how to write happiness much. My eyes always on the hardness, the strangeness of her. He dies six years into their life.

When Empress Messalina Potentially Decides the Son of Agrippina And Agrippina Herself A Threat
(47 c.e., Rome)

Eight hundred years after Romulus held
his brother to stillness   Emperor Claudius

hosts secular games   There is the opening
of throats of animals   Fifty-some women

and children sing Sapphic Horace   *ludos*
ter die claro totiensque grata   nocte frequentis

There a Troy Pageant with sons   a parade
of youths   future politicians on horseback

Britannicus moves by   and applause
for the emperor's boy   Agrippina alone

regal in the stands   crowds seeing her   the twice-
widow   Son so like her   like Germanicus

face wide brows flaring to the temples
They cheer for Germanicus and his blood

in the boy's body so shaped   The blood
in Germanicus's brother Claudius not

nearly as fine   The boy's dappled stud
prances   They call out at the reincarnation

. . .

The games's source   a man praying
for ill children   The cure in a voice

he hears   The games's style of sacrifice
in the healed children's dreams

This is important as Agrippina still had pull in Rome, even as a widow, due to the general love of her father, Germanicus (now-Emperor Claudius's brother). Agrippina's son was thus quickly beloved in this public place. Empress Messalina perhaps saw power for herself and her son Britannicus, she and Agrippina strange mirrors of each other—at least this is how the annals portray them.

The Attempted Assassination of Agrippina's Son During Sleep

(47 c.e., *Antium*)

Messalina sends a man who moves
soundless into the room   He reaches
pets the neck to keep sleep on the face

until around the throat a slow hardening
Small coughs finally   eyes   as hands
closing around pulling the boy

to blotted edges   dullness   sparks
Then a curling flash   snake silvery
from a cushion   The man's look on scales

glinting and   in the terror's rush   flees
The child crawls to his mother hands on throat
rasping   What fear she must have felt then . . .

Or perhaps all rumor   one Agrippina bent—
the sources make it impossible to know   Where
is there no bias?   Does such a chronicle exist?

Allow me to choose the one in which I see
Agrippina set the snakeskin in gold   work it up
her son's right arm to protect him when she cannot

This bracelet he throws away years later in a fit
of rage *and afterwards* one historian writes
in the time of his extremity sought it again in vain

The Vatican Museum

Many stone Emperor Claudiuses around. Here huge as Jupiter, and markedly muscled despite the emperor's age and habits. He raises a thing broken off, the other hand reaches out with a plate. A large leafy diadem around his head, robe dipped then thrown over his shoulder as a god might. At his feet, a flat-headed eagle, looking upward and expectant like a dog.

A bust of Claudius looks simple, but its placard complicates—tells it had been Caligula once, severed from a body on a throne and "reworked." *This can be detected in the relatively smaller proportions of the face compared to the neck and the presence of a double fringe over the forehead, the upper one undoubtedly being left over from the previous portrait.* Incredulous, I think, How does a double-bang layer tell all that? Then, unavoidable, un-unseeable. The face petite between the ears, the large hair around it. When to trust the historical narrative? When is it not hostile to exposure?

Once emperor, Claudius found a chest filled with the many poisons Caligula had cultivated and kept. The new emperor ordered it thrown into the sea, which *so infected it as to kill the fish, which were thrown up by the tide upon the neighboring shores.*

The victor's perspective is so dominating, a modern historian writes, *that it is easier to be suspicious of the standard line than to replace it.*

¤

Caligula was recarved into others after his death, for he was sentenced to damnatio memoriae—condemnation of memory, oblivion, erasure of. To redact a human from history, chisel their name to flatness. Painted faces were smudged into blurring, blotches hovering above bodies. This punishment was cast upon the most terrible of traitors by the Senate, along with a death sentence. This excision from memory was considered worse than forced suicide. Livilla was the first woman in the imperial family to receive it, Messalina the second.

What of what's left out, simply? Or like Agrippina—whittled away by time, the lack of interest in copying words she wrote.

Years after the moment Claudius becomes emperor, she wrote her de vita eius ("on her life"). Emperors and statesmen wrote their de vita sua, populated them with tales of their political ascents and military conquests. Agrippina describes giving birth. While they write of battles, she tells us her son was breech—and that they both lived. We only know this from Pliny's reference to her de vita eius. Her words are lost, uncopied. Even Tacitus's work becomes a fragment the moment he starts to tell us more about Agrippina.

Her brother Caligula was expunged—but not fully. Claudius halted it.

Agrippina the Younger's Marriage to Emperor Claudius
A Braiding of Split Imperial Branches

(49 C.E., Rome)

Agrippina and Claudius wed on New Year's Day

a bright flame of veil falls across her white tunic

cinched with knotted wool   Away at the Lake

of Nemi   pontiffs come upon the Grove

of Diana   set a sheaf of golden wheat

pull back the velveteen chin of a long-

eared ewe to slit her neck before the carved

sculpture of the goddess as three robed figures

for this strange marriage of close kin

Sheep's blood speckles the grain there—

the goddess's six stone arms slung around one another

This is important as Empress Messalina perhaps wanted another politician in the emperor's seat—and planned with him to grasp it while Emperor Claudius was away. Or perhaps she staged a Bacchic party with a lover rather than a coup. Claudius's trusted assistant Narcissus, a formerly enslaved man, ultimately ordered Messalina's execution without Claudius's permission—yet received no punishment. This gave Agrippina an opening she had probably not thought possible. Claudius was her uncle, and no such incestuous union had yet taken place.

Agrippina the Younger
Once with Power
Does What She Has Long Desired
(49 c.e., Rome)

Stars prick into being   Four slaves
carry sister Livilla's ashes set the urn

in a mausoleum niche   Agrippina
slow behind   Having lodged it

the slaves move away   Agrippina there
turns a vessel   pouring into an opening

at the urn's top   listens to
the silvery hiss of wine hitting ash

In her mind   Livilla alive when small—
as small as the urn that holds her ash-self

Agrippina's eyes set on honey stone   tracing
the alabaster's veins   cream and ice

branching around ashes   moving
through the etched   HIC CREMATUS EST

The Material
Marital
Benefits
For Empress Agrippina
(49 c.e., Rome)

The couple stamped
in gold   infinitely

moves from hands
to other hands   A holy

carriage carved   Her
carpentum of blond wood

its draped fabric ceiling
The interior cushions   cloths

embroidered with pearls
gold   precious stones

Her son now Claudius's son—
successor   future emperor

See her in repose   The cozy
grandeur cuddled up around her

eyes on the precise cloth   A breath
of certainty so few of us know

as she is drawn through the city
by two fine reddish mules

The Forum

This was a bog the Romans drained to hardness. Much later, wind moved earth in, slowly but fully, until the Forum was lost. This center dip between hills forgotten. For centuries, it was a grazing place. A J. M. W. Turner painting shows goats picking along the edges, goatherds's tossed cloaks on large tumbled marble pieces. It was dubbed Campo Vaccino (Cow Field), for it was that until concerted excavation.

Before the cows, here were meetings, political decisions, the bank, the temples where animals were slit throats for gods, enemy heads stuck in the rostra. The place of triumphal marches miles long, orations for the dead, bustling center, site of the Temple of Vesta, kindling lost in raging fire (fire after fire). My mind on that history, but here Turner includes the Colosseum pale and damaged in the background, hazy, and I wonder what it is to live in a place with such enormous ruins. With columns standing, some solitary, over fifty feet high, and chunks of marble so large many horses were all that might move them. How to engage with a place, with what you can't build upon? What use of it? Perhaps it is all an uninspired metaphor for what I am up to—trying to dig through the palimpsest of time, holding different artifacts up to the light to discern their use.

Many walls here are cobbled of ancient stone, their original dates carved in. Nero once built an enormous bronze statue of himself. It was later pulled down and pried apart for the metal.

The Celtic Chieftain Caratacus Captured Brought to Rome in Chains Paraded Before the Masses
(51 c.e., Rome)

His vestments of pelt and gold stripped
so the cerulean ink seen snaking across
his fine arms and chest in the daylight

Caratacus his family other Celts
push along in slow procession   Known
for slippery evasions in Welsh mountains

his undeniable fame brings Romans out
The imperial couple watches from two daises
just higher than the bunched heads

Caratacus stops there where he bows
to the emperor as is custom   then
raises himself and bows to the empress

Agrippina looks down at the man of such
power bending toward the earth before her
and a dark joy glitters up through her

▽

If you'd been born a century ago, that could've been your destiny, even if you were a good girl. Starving to death in someone's tomb. Cheating your way into a better life.
    —TRISHA LOW QUOTING HER GRANDMOTHER ON EMPRESS WU ZETIAN,
    A ROYAL CONCUBINE SO FORMIDABLE SHE BECAME THE FIRST AND,
    THUS FAR, ONLY FEMALE SOVEREIGN OF CHINA (690–750 C.E.)

The Augustan Sanctuary and Residential Complex

Emperor Augustus decided to leave his residence in the Forum and claimed the house of an orator in the Palatine. There was construction there until the spot was struck by lightning, so Augustus declared it public—the area holy, a place of Apollo worship. A later emperor filled it all in with dirt. The burial left the frescoes still bright and whole. Some are recent assembly work from small, crushed, egg-like parts. But whatever, full or in pieces, had fallen face down—buried by time or dictate.

Archaeologists do this now to save things. They begin excavation until money runs out, then a careful returning. This protects from thieves, the elements. Augustus's stable, for example, was found while digging a parking lot. Money located for preservation as the two thousandth anniversary of Augustus's death approached, then that money lost. So archaeologists began *covering the remains of Augustus's marbled stables with waterproof cloths, ready for reburial, left for future generations to discover.*

But what about what never made it? Received not even an ounce of such care? That which was exposed to whatever strips it to nothing? Or, even worse, contorts it to confusion for whomever finds it? We don't even know where Agrippina is fucking buried.

¤

A dark placard with white text upright under a tree reads: *This was an area of aristocratic houses, with luxurious wall and floor decorations, of which significant remains survive to give us an idea of how the Palatine looked when it was home to Rome's most powerful men.*

Augustus stated of Rome: *Urbem latericium invenit, marmoream reliquit.* The translations of this vary. My try: *I found a city of brick, leave it one of marble.*

Rome's most powerful MEN—a dodge I see over and over again.

Suetonius writes of Emperor Augustus as a child, *As soon as he began to talk, it chanced that the frogs were making great noise at his grandfather's country place. He bade them be silent, and they say no frog has ever croaked there.*

Augustus's rule was, according to one historian, the *blueprint that every emperor for the next 200 years was judged.* His wife Livia's marks on this blueprint disregarded, diminished, and forgotten.

¤

The literature that exists from ancient Rome was what medieval monks and Islamic scholars thought important enough to transcribe by hand.

I am sick over the fact that Agrippina wrote three memoirs during her exile from Rome by Nero. They described her life and the lives of each of her parent's families. These memoirs disappeared in the chaos of time. One historian calls this *one of the saddest losses of classical literature.*

I don't know who said this. Maybe it's no one. Maybe it's me. Augustus also had one that didn't survive, but he has plenty.

Future Emperor Nero Assumes the Toga Virilis His Role as Adult

(51 c.e., *Palatine Hill, Rome*)

The brass Lar   god of the house   dotted
in fresh flowers   its boyish curls calf boots

Metal fabric fans at the high-girted tunic
as in air   Its arm raises a horn-shaped rhyton

tapering into a goat   Nero lifts from his neck
the gold amulet strung on leather   weighted

there since infancy   He sets it in the bowl
entwined in the Lar's reaching fingers

Then his praetexta tunic off   its thick purple edging
running around the white   The new cloth brought

over the head by Emperor Claudius   the toga virilis
white only   curled over the body in mature perfection

They go to the small shrine of Minerva's room to leave
a coin to her   as all new men have for centuries

I wonder about the coins to Minerva those pressed
into splayed hands en route to the banquet after

Perhaps this defines a man—   the placement
of gold into the palms of others   as is their pleasure

The Colosseum

I don't go. I don't care. What is there for me? But I walk past it, often. It is impressive in its size. Named for the colossal bronze statue Nero built of himself, the vast amphitheater later *pointedly built on the site that had once belonged to Nero's private park.* The lines curl outside, men in cheap fabric armor cozy up to tourists for photos. And—have fun. I am not fun. I want no vision of the deaths in it and the cheering. The most interesting fact I learn is it was once filled with hundreds of varieties of plants from all over the Roman Empire, from what was carried in the bellies of animals killed there (flamingos, hyenas), the seedy fruits they ate. The gory dirt sprouted all the colors and green shapes otherwise foreign to the city. But those plants don't exist there now. All those I care for were dead when they started stacking the building's limestone.

But it trails me all over. Look at something from another vantage, and it hovers in the distance. Enormous, pale, pocked—like a dry honeycomb cracked open.

The Death of Emperor Claudius at Age Sixty-Three In Its Multitudinous Truths
(53 c.e., Rome)

Agrippina has the woman Locusta mix
a slow poison   then handed to his taster who

spreads it quietly on the largest mushroom—
a shining fan on his plate   At the banquet

he seated drunk full again gut hurting
as was common but here without speech

Shits or vomits   then a bit better
Taken to his room   where a doctor

(bought) pushes the quick-poison-
dipped feather edge down his throat

in guise of purging   Or the doctor
laces healing soup   Or there is malaria

heart failure or gastroenteritis But death
and Agrippina fending knowledge of it

She orders bulletins on pickets
to report his progress gaining

She keeps his children away in rooms
Packs Claudius with blankets   poultices

to stave stiffening for time to rally allies
Or for the death on an auspicious day

No matter   for by the next noon
Nero is on a platform   hailed into power

The Brief Period of Agrippina Holding Total Power Through Her Emperor-Son
(53–54 C.E., Rome)

A new doorway built   a curtain
set there so unseen   The chair
behind that   And she entered

the palace's Senate room silently
seated   ear out   directing the empire
this way   Nero's spoken words

her words   Seneca's   her tongue
through his mouth   And the empire
is thus ruled into some peace as

she had with Claudius   but further
Now   the throne is hers   glory
in the walking into her power

But soon the hairlines are pried
to fissure by Seneca   Burrus
How quickly Agrippina's catch

on the reins begins
to slide   silk on silk
small bursts of slipping

This is important as Britannicus was a threat to his stepbrother Nero's power. Agrippina had possibly tried to push Britannicus into the emperor's seat despite his seizures and illness. Nero realized an imperial precedent of patricide and the number of other potential successors had dwindled. Nero wanted Agrippina gone, sent her away—and then called off her guards. A punishment of maddening quiet.

The Island of Capri

In a jokey fake toy commercial for the film *Caligula*, a boy with titular toy in hand says, *I shall marry you, Sister!* A mother is nearby, arm on an olive tree. She laughs to herself, winks at the camera. In the films and books I force-feed myself, many figures are meant to be read as perverted. They're all having sex with the wrong people (siblings, parents) in the Roman annals too, so it's not from nowhere. The claim of deviant sex was a lazy way to slander, historically. The wild part is that these claims have endured.

So in the recent movies and novels on this time, everyone fucks each other too. They gorge on meals to illustrate excess. As if orgies don't happen now, people don't eat for pleasure—and, truly, blessings upon those who do. These sexual exploits, manipulations, murders all are meant to tell us: You are not these people. You live in a better time. But to look and think, *Not I. Not us, now*, is a joke. Their behavior is hardly novel or foreign. Power, desire—nothing has changed. Neither has abuse.

The mute freak is a figure of otherness upon which the spectators could displace anxieties and uncertainties about their own identities, writes one scholar. I think of all the words Agrippina penned, rendered silent by those words's destruction.

Watching *Caligula*, I roll my eyes at the incest, the purposefully absurd wig on Tiberius's head. I never thought these people were freaks. I just wanted to know what situation resulted in a powerful woman being assassinated by her son. How afterward maybe he looked at her uterus (what Aretaeus called the *animal within the animal*), but probably not. I will later learn this is an invention beyond even the annals—in art beginning only in the fifteenth century. But the macabre story of Agrippina's death hounded me. Then I fell into the void of her existence in her own life's story.

While we are gripped by their dramas, these people largely focused on power. Tiberius's and Caligula's known obsession with power makes a sort of sense. Rather than the former Republic, the empire made a single mind capable of controlling its entirety, the borders of which spread from what is now India to

Spain, from Egypt to the shores of France. And that man's mind making decisions impacting multitudes often rested close to a woman's. And who knows what turned inside there? The senators and public wondered. They grew worried, they fixated.

Agrippina, like Livia before her, saw the potential such proximity allowed. It became her obsession too—how to position herself so she might sway, even control. She saw more success than almost any other woman in ancient Roman history, save for Livia (an empress for thirty-nine years, and one who could apparently bend her the ear of her husband, Augustus).

Perhaps this idea that I "fell into the void" of Agrippina's existence is reductive. Maybe it was because I had undiagnosed depression at the time, which can provoke obsessions of different sorts. But something far bigger than that tipped me into that void and, before that, made me edge ever closer. Here was a woman who lived in a society that treated her like a second-class citizen. This was transmitted to her implicitly and explicitly throughout her life and in the literature after her murder. In essence, her plight felt familiar. Yet she was ambitious and had things she could exploit (her mind, her lineage, her ability to have a male child) in order to pursue her aims. And exploit them she did—until she realized her impossible quest for power. She got further than many even dared to begin to hope.

Yet it's possible I stared into the dark boundless space of her life because, while I didn't know it yet, its narrative elements might also serve as a lesson—if one looked closely enough. So, I peer. I learn that power rarely promises safety if your society generally maligns an element of your indelible identity. That the person most likely to cut a woman into pieces is a man to whom she is close. That the belief you can exploit a system built to exploit you is, ultimately, a farce—your successes can be undone in an instant. That your gains will come at an enormous cost, which may be invisible to you until it's too late. That your existence can be manipulated both during your life and after death. And that all of this has been true for thousands of years.

By the second half of *Caligula*, I write down, *Where the fuck is Agrippina?* The filmmakers are as predictable as ever—she never arrives.

The First Assassination Attempt on Agrippina by Her Son, Emperor Nero

(58 c.e., Rome)

She takes the cup
eyes up as she drinks

the cherry laurel water—
cyanide sapped from pits

Nero does not realize she
kills men with mushrooms

cooked in aconite
poisoned feather tips

eased down their throats
She drains the cup   Eyes

blink into hellebore buds
lungs puff—pink datura trumpets

spray of colchicum for a heart
guts tangled thapsia stalks

Her dark tongue then the very
cherry laurel leaf

smelling of almonds
wide and inviting

The Second Assassination Attempt on Agrippina by Her Son the Emperor Nero

(59 c.e., *Bay of Baiae*)

After the oarsmen set it on fire
the boat's prow curls in like a fern

A lead ceiling drops
hits the keep   which

yawns   opens to water
Why not push this

absurdity further?
Wood hinges inward

sails chirring   The stem
pleats again and again—

all according to plan
until it stills   a little box

Agrippina floats through water
Let volcanoes in the depths

erupt as she passes until
she toes the nearby shore

where a crowd has gathered
They chant her name

spread her out on the sand
weave raw twigs through her hair

rub oil into her skin   kiss
her breasts pour milk and wine

into her mouth while
the boat empty burns

During the Assassination Attempt on Agrippina in Which Her Maid, Acerronia, Tries to Survive

(59 C.E., *Bay of Baiae*)

Acerronia falls through the open floor
Clinging to the boat's side   she calls

for aid   *I am Agrippina!*   sure the lie
will cloak her with power   safety

Men hear   and find her—
bludgeon her with oars and poles

until she breaks into parts   The blood
and the water mixing together

    . . .

I see Agrippina wait   make her
way through the quiet dark eddy

The Assassination of Agrippina

(59 c.e., *Bay of Baiae*)

The ship a tall flame on water
Agrippina drags herself onto shore

covered in sand and water greens
She pants on her back awhile

A light there on her eyes—
she opens sees a bright blade

There is no stopping what has
already happened   A band latches

on my throat   I want her to have
power of command here too

to slow the inevitable
down to tenderness

Wait she says
and he does

They sit cross-legged
telling of things—every

moment that led to this one
But time passes

There is no more to tell   Agrippina
grows quiet   *I suppose you*

should kill me   The man looks away
Here she says   trains the knife

on her womb   *Do it here so*
maybe he too will feel it

Emperor Nero After the Assassination of His Mother, Agrippina
(59 c.e., Bay of Baiae)

Her soul whistles out
until Nero seals the lips

pushes her lids shut
His office fills with letters

of praise   Her corpse laid
on a dining couch   then set

on fire—gold fabric whips
sparks around thinning flesh

In the pyre Nero sees what will return
each night   curling from her open tomb

into his bed—what the magi
cannot exorcise—Agrippina

with astrologers who foretell
her death   and Agrippina's reply:

Let him kill me
as long as he reigns

One ancient historian
writes that Nero *was hounded*

by his mother's ghost and by the whips
and blazing torches of the Furies

So perhaps Nero learned
death does not snuff power

It can manifest itself
in innumerable shapes

Give me great power   even brief
Even if death is the cost

The Bay of Baiae

Her tomb is in an unknown spot, and I don't make it to the site of her assassination. On the map it is a little curl of water just edging up the coast from her quasi-exile at Misenum. There are dashed lines marking boat paths. This, where Caligula rode a horse on water, then where Nero called Agrippina from her villa for the goddess Minerva. There were whispers of a plot, so she exercised caution. Nero met her on the shore (sand? rocks?). He was full of affection, pointed to a ship, beautiful, decorated for her. But she, perhaps wary, was instead carried on a litter by slaves to dinner. The food and love there, a playfulness. Her advice and him seeming to take it. A long embrace and his looking at her with a lost feeling. *Possibly as a final touch of hypocrisy,* Tacitus writes, *or possibly the last look upon his doomed mother gave pause even to that brutal spirit.* She, so convinced, boarded the ship made for sinking. Maybe I am more willing to consider this portrayal as there were enslaved people, maids, many eyes there to relay what transpired to others.

In one long, epic movie I watch over two nights, Agrippina is already dead. She's barely mentioned at the start as murdered. *Great,* I think, ready to write off the film as a waste of time. I hate the movie the first night, want the creep of a protagonist to die. For the second night, I think *fuck it,* get stoned—and find it brilliant. I'm grateful to see the fire of Rome and all its chaos, think the actor playing Nero is perhaps a genius. Agrippina comes up once in the second half, with an uncharacteristic close-up on Nero. His nostrils flare as he says it was necessary to kill her. One contemporary poet assumes the voice of Nero, writing of Agrippina, *She plotted to be the mother to the whole world / She died and was transformed into mud / Mud that stinks so much it stings the eyes and nose / And all credit for casting her into mud / Belongs to me.*

Tacitus tells us that, after Agrippina's murder, inauspicious signs fell upon Rome: *A woman gave birth to a serpent, another was killed by a thunderbolt in the embraces of her husband; the sun, again, was suddenly obscured.* And yet— The events *so little marked the concern of the gods that Nero continued for years in his empire and his crimes.*

The Uprising of Over 200,000 Tribespeople Led by Tribal Queen Boudica For Her Husband's Naming His Two Daughters (and Nero) as Heirs When She Became a Widow

(61 c.e., Britannia)

Centurions lash the queen
with leather   rape the princesses

So Boudica gathers her tribe and another
Her daughters in her chariot   her spear close

Tall with hair tawny to the waist   variegated tunic
the large cloak shut with a circle of silver

a heavy torc of gold twisted at her neck
The tribes move through settlements with fire

cut throats   string up bodies   temples all apart
So fell Camulodunum   Verulamium   Londinium

Roman corpses in tens of thousands
When facing Nero's army over a road   thick

woods behind Boudica speaks *I am fighting as a human*
for my stolen freedom   bruised body   enraged daughters

As for you men   go ahead and live—
and be slaves   Then she lets a coney hare

from her tunic its path a guide to clashing glitter
of metals   But soon their wood is in pieces   hooves

pull at gory muck   Boudica sees her warriors's
deaths   and her own   in the blood

so she tongues down a dark seed of poison
Her death is hers and belongs to no man

Agrippina is Boudica's shadow   A woman
powerful   so certain of her cause   self   and yet—

. . .

With this victory of Roman suppression
Nero closes the gates of the Temple of Janus *as a sign*

that no war was left anywhere   But the signs remain
Centuries later a clutch of precious items   body parts

The Boudica hoard includes a sword-sliced
kneecap   a jawbone splintered by metal

These are likely Roman parts   We see some deaths
here   now   in the dirt   The earth contains her mark

Death doesn't pinch off the realities of influence—
the earth witnesses   turns up what is buried

for us to recognize   What more
might time give?

This is important as it was a woman's bloody claim for power and the Roman response was brutal. It was an outsized punishment for a decree that broke up Nero's power in a far-flung place. This quelled uprising was an undeniable success for Nero before a long, clear decline.

The Great Fire of Rome
(64 c.e.)

It starts at the Circus   clambers up
the hills   Wall-less parts keep it taking

quarter upon quarter   The people
rush elsewhere only to face more flames

Some collapse prone in grasslands   Some linger
for those caught up   and so caught themselves

Days later most everything is in ashy bits
hot to touch   Then it breaks out again

to take a temple and more   Nero opens
the Field of Mars for those on the street

gives food   incurs the cost himself
Perhaps this the source of his damnation

in history—tending to the public and enraging
the wealthy   But wonders at its starting   Nero

the cause maybe   He names the source:
Christians   begins their tortures to silence rumor

A brilliant streak of comet hovers in the sky
for days   then weeks of lightning cracking

One man finds a calf dead in a ditch
its head and hoof fused together

Nero's Domus Aurea

The fire raged a week before running out of fuel, during which time Nero gave a musical performance in Antium, far from Rome—hence the long-standing description of the emperor at his lyre during the disaster. I watch *Home Alone* for the first time in decades and it's even there. The pizza delivery from Little Nero's Pizza, tagline: *no fiddlin' around*. (This detail is a nettling inaccuracy, as fiddles didn't exist until centuries after Nero's death—it was probably a cithara.)

After this fire's vast fanning, Nero built a palace with obsession. It was as large as a grove—and there were groves. A lake dug, vineyards, a pasture. Animals, wild and tame, meandered. The building itself was room after room after room with no latrine or bed, for it was not for living. A celestial ceiling cranked into motion by enslaved people. Rose petals dropped from upturned ivory panels, the petals to such extremity they once smothered a guest. There was a nymphaeum dedicated to Ulysses. Light off its water glanced the glass mosaic ceiling. There was an enormous pond with flitting fish. According to Suetonius, Nero said, when the palace was finished, he was *at last beginning to be housed like a human being.*

Here were the first mosaics on ceilings ever. One is a face, half gone, hair curling and colored like dull flames, the single orange eye rolled upward. The head and part of a gray snake's body calm there near the eye.

As I move through it, a guide points to a bright square the size of my hand up high on the wall. Perfect clarity amid grime. It is a window into a time before, the preservationists's work done there alone. When I ask why so small, she explains a lack of money. This in a place that Suetonius introduces by saying, *There was nothing however in which Nero was more ruinously prodigal than in building.* Agrippina, excellent with money, never would have allowed it.

Another emperor covered it all in earth. It was found centuries later when a young man fell into the dirt and, seeing the work, brought others who used ladders of rope and wood to go down. Michelangelo and Raphael scratched their names on a wall, but I don't ever find that. Indeed, these frescoes inspired the Renaissance painters, when they began to render Agrippina's corpse under Nero's probing eye.

¤

Years later, an exhibition on Nero is up at the British Museum. Its curator states, *He was a spoiled young aristocrat. But he wasn't a monster.* I think, Bullshit. One review of the exhibition mentions Agrippina in the second sentence, and I am awash with a feeling of tardy recognition. It claims her remark *Strike my womb* is actually from *Oedipus.* The author writes, *Seneca wrote the play around the time of Nero's rule, and it's possible that his retelling of the mythic story was inspired by the actual manner of Agrippina's death.* But—and I disagree before I read anything else. I give it to her, considering none of her many words survived.

The Death of Emperor Nero
(68 c.e., Rome)

Visions in sleep start   Dead wife Octavia dragging
him by the hair into shadow   He sees himself
blanketed in ants with their silvery wings endless
Or feels his way through darkness   then a light
on the mausoleum   its doors flung apart
Armies begin to name fidelity to others
Nero tries to rally tribunes   centurions
who do nothing—quote Virgil on death
One night he sleeps in the palatial garden
awakens to silence   bodyguards gone
He calls out into quiet   nudges doors to rooms
Screams for any hand to kill him a gladiator
any other   Nothing   *Then I have no friend
or enemy left* he tells no one   But there an ally
and a freedman and there his boy-wife Sporus
Nero dressed rattily on a horse to a villa
outside the city   His abettor offers a hole
for hiding but Nero fears being in the earth
while alive   A way being dug under walls so
unseen by the villa's slaves   Nero prone in shrubs
birdsong and gusts through trees rattle him into fear
Finally he gropes through dirt and is inside
on the ally's couch rests there   *The world is losing
a rare artist* he says to the ceiling   A letter comes
with knowing him there   Nero named enemy
of the state to be met with ancient punishment
Nero not knowing what   and the friends tell
of his body bared   neck between posts beaten
with cane until bleeding out   Nero finds and lifts
a dagger up trembles at cane death   knife death
Asks for someone to suicide with him to guide
for Sporus to wail   Hooves hit close earth

and he pushes the blade in his throat
another helps press   A centurion bounds in
tosses his cloak to stanch and give death later
Nero thinks otherwise   *So loyal—but too late*

. . .

Claudia Ecloge   the enslaved woman
who nursed Nero buries him   She nursed his body
then buried it   Perhaps she was tender with him
Perhaps completing a simple duty   Who knows her feelings
Soon the Roman people take to the streets as those
freed from slavery   And yet for a time impostors
claim to be Nero   alive   For months some unseen
acolytes set flowers on his tomb   The tomb of his father
in sight of the grand   mausoleum   that line fully cut

The Mausoleum of Augustus

Rome was sacked six times. In 410 c.e., it was the Visigoths. Not the first, but terrifying and thorough. Saint Jerome wrote, *My voice sticks in my throat, and, as I dictate, sobs choke my utterance. The City that had taken the whole world was itself taken.*

Knowing his doom, a Roman man waited in armor on a chair. The Visigoths entered and saw him and thought him a statue—until he sprang into action, dying honorably. (Yet who survived this and told it? Wrote it down?)

They looted it all—including the centuries-old mausoleum, pulling the goods from its crypts, busting marble so the imperial ashes poured and rolled through the air and over each other. They flung the bones around.

The Tiber took the mausoleum next, circled it in its silt, made it invisible. Buried for long enough that generations thought for good.

Elsewhere

Sometime later, near home, I go to a place made of oil money. Oklahoma-Kuwait crude paid. A man who said, *The meek shall inherit the earth, but not its mineral rights* built Roman inner and outer peristyles with black stone sculptures nestled in English ivy. He collected statues, coins, jewelry. He had so many objects, Italy charged he owned it all only through centuries-old looting—and demanded their return. It is warm here as in Rome, the paintings on peristyle walls in Roman design with masks in ribbons and small creatures above angled architectural shapes.

Not all of the figures I want, but some. The head of Tiberius, mouth set, had been on a random nude body. So it was cut off and lodged on a metal rod into a dark cube of stone. Augustus and Nero pressed into gold money. Augustus looking calm and modern with no lettering, while Nero bears a laurel, his neck cartoonishly thick. Then more stone heads in a large room with space around. One historian reminds, *Ask yourself whenever you're looking at something like this treasure: Who made it? Who cleaned it?* I think of the working hands for these figures as I eye Livia, serene, with nose worn to nostrils, half the head missing starting at the temple. Sunlight falls nicely from the center on Caligula, then on Augustus with hair in hooks on the brow. And there, to the side, is Agrippina. Her family in a kind of order. The marble of her is formed with a slight smile, hair tight curls from a center part, then spun on the sides to a tether broken before meeting, hair on the back calm. It is from something larger, a body lost to time.

Addendum—Livilla's Urn

It is a dangerous myth that we are better historians than our predecessors.

—MARY BEARD

I went in search of Livilla and the alabaster that held her ashes—to see this urn from 47 C.E. in person. My proposal for the grant that paid my way to Rome hinged on this object. For, despite the incredible work of everything from books to digital archives to blogs, this urn seemed lost in a void. I wanted to describe it accurately. From books, I knew the alabaster was cream colored with icy veins. Based on when it was made, I knew that etched on its side it likely said HIC CREMATUS EST and it was the shape of an ornately carved house, with a slot at the top for pouring milk and wine onto the ashes. But perhaps not. Perhaps none of these attributes. That was what the books described, but nothing more.

I picked a horrible time to go to the Vatican Museum. The urn was there—that I knew. I needed to get in, and my days in Rome were disappearing quickly, so I went when tickets were available. The crowd of people was such that, even with my advanced booking, I was caught up within the teeming crowd. Vatican maps are inscrutable—like a metro map lacking the details of how far apart different stops are located or even where they are. Just different destinations in a kind of shape, a rough order. Considering the tourist's experience of this museum, this is an unsurprising curatorial decision. Most people move in a single direction without regard for their options. I felt like I was in a pumping heart. Pushed through this circuit with no possibility of alternative routes, I was terrified that at any moment I might surge past the urn. People weren't looking at much, generally. For most, these sculptures and artifacts are what you pass on the way to the Sistine Chapel, which is just an obligatory stop before going on to something else in the city.

¤

In ancient Rome, when someone dies, loved ones gather. The closest family member closes the eyes and kisses the mouth. The body is placed on a dirt floor, just as when a Roman baby is born. For the wealthy, enslaved people wash the body. Dress it in oil and fine clothes and place it for people to view in the home, feet facing the door. There is no embalming. Perfumey herbs are laid out. In the mouth or on each of the eyes is a coin—Charon's obol—to get them over water and into the underworld.

¤

From my research, I believed Livilla's urn was located in the Gregorian Etruscan wing. I searched for the wing while being pushed through rooms and passageways along with the hundreds of other Vatican visitors, my eyes scanning for the wing's marker. In the main rooms were busts and tile mosaics and Nero's grand bathtub carved from porphyry (one of the museum's most valuable artifacts). When facing a long hallway with row after row of Roman statues and urns with no placards or explanation beyond an inventory number, I began to panic. I might unknowingly pass the urn. I asked a guard, who had never heard of it. He could only tell me I was not in the right wing—the language barrier stopped us there. I looped back to the outdoor courtyard to think. I asked another guard—"Upstairs." I had just been upstairs but perhaps I had missed a turn. I went back into the throng, pushed along until again came the pang of worry that I had missed something. I fought back through the crowd out to the courtyard once more where I had space to breathe. I found a third guard and asked again. He worked his forehead a bit with his fingers and then remembered that the Gregorian Etruscan wing is often closed in the afternoons. It was on the third floor. My gut sank as I moved through the rooms and found the wing, indeed, cordoned off. I peeked through the locked metal-framed glass doors and spied the display cases filled with wares of antiquity. Wrung out, I walked through the major arteries of the building, looked at other artifacts. Eventually I sat, face upward, gazing at the Sistine Chapel. An audio guide piped information into my ear, making me feel like the planning and hours and museum fee were perhaps not all for nothing.

¤

After some days, there is a procession through Roman streets. At the very least, there are flute players. The procession's grandness depends on the wealth of the dead—with more money comes more living bodies that surround the cortege. The body is on a pallet, borne by male family members dressed in grays and browns. Female relatives follow in white. Actors bear imagines—ancestral masks of the relatives of the deceased. There are mimes and musicians. Women who weep for pay tear out their hair in clumps. The procession in death is often larger than that of a wedding.

☒

Once I got back to my flat, I emailed the Vatican help desk. I attempted to make clear my (actually flimsy) importance and the validity of my need to access the Etruscan wing. I had a grant specifically to see this object. I needed the details of the Etruscan's hours of operation. In a few hours, I received a response referring me to another office. From this point on, I found myself in awe of Vatican bureaucracy (or at least that of its museum). The second office responded promptly the next morning. They required a letter from my department in order to provide me one hour of free access to the wing I required for my research. I quickly supplied this document, and they provided me a time and instructions. Upon returning to the Vatican Museum, the man at the information desk immediately knew who I was. I watched as he filled out a special permission sheet. (A Vatican form bearing a SPECIAL PERMISSION stamp by my name is ephemera I am pained to not hold in my personal archive.) The museum information desk staff member called over a guard, and I was escorted past the crowds. I clicked up the marble stairs, and a guard from within the Gregorian Etruscan wing keyed open the deadbolt for our entry. This entire process, from my first email that morning to the opening of the desired locked door, took no more than three hours.

I moved through the wing with my personal guard trailing behind. Some of the wing's oldest artifacts there were indeed urns—from thousands and thousands of years ago. Dark, wide-lipped vases with mushroom cap lids to keep the remains within. Others looked like thatched huts. Some were mud, some bronze. The human interest in the dead, the desire to burn a body up and place it somewhere—the importance of that somewhere—has existed for ages. I knew this, and I know it is hardly limited to the West. But when you're looking specifically for an urn, you start to look at all urns differently. The clock was ticking on my hour in the wing, so I pushed on past very ancient materials—I needed to reach the first half of the first century C.E. There was a room of alabaster marble urns with ornate narrative carvings on their sides. These were a bit longer than my forearm. The lids of each bore a reclining body, partially raised up, the face looking outward. These were dated second to third century B.C.E. Then second century B.C.E. I found one that didn't look too different from the others in the room, but the placard dated it from the "latter half of first century B.C." and I felt myself tremble for its closeness to the date of the urn I wanted to see, for Livilla died in the mid-first century C.E. I realized that if I did find Livilla's urn, I would weep in front of it, alone, save for a bewildered guard nearby.

¤

Eulogies are also made during the procession. For men, mostly. For the very important, the procession pauses at the Forum for those to speak to the public of the dead, from a platform. Speeches are solely to praise—one was not to speak ill of the dead. The poor likely made speeches of love, but there is no record there.

¤

This impulse to cry before Livilla's urn wasn't because of the wonder of locating an elusive object as an emotional researcher—though that may have been a small part of it. That morning, I had gotten word my uncle had died during the Roman night as I slept. Just a few weeks prior, we received news that his cancer, which had been in full remission not two months ago, had returned. But there was a chance. Then it was back, and everywhere. I had run all over Rome for days, hitting the locations I was compelled to see for my research, worrying over the chance of bad news and needing to be called away. I held on to my tasks fiercely, as one might the neck of a bolting horse. I saved the Vatican for last, as I thought it would be the easiest of my research locations—a puzzle already solved before my arrival.

I had not yet cried over my uncle's death that day, feeling numb and searching for a mission. The Vatican provided, with its staff's magnificent promptness. So I found myself pausing over these vessels of death—this stone and bronze that survived longer than the ash remains they once contained.

I made a ring around the room, looked closely at the dates on the small laminated placards, the translations of the carved inscriptions. Nothing. Nothing after Christ's death—that definitive marker. I pushed on to a room with two full-body sarcophagi in red clay from Tuscany, their lids with life-size depictions of the dead, eyes wide and vacant as I know the dead can stare before one gently holds the eyelids shut. One full clay body was cracked in half at the hips, and I was startled by how deeply this damage pricked me.

I began to grow desperate. I went from vessel to vessel, room to room, and could not find Livilla's urn. I enlisted the help of my guard. We swept through the whole Etruscan wing again as a team—no luck. He popped into the wing's office and pulled down a large blue binder, leafing through what was a surprisingly casual photo album of the objects within the Etruscan, but this gave us nothing. I began to think I must have passed it in another wing when I wandered through the museum the other day. In one wing there were many urns on pedestals without markers other than numbers. Hundreds and hundreds. My guard shrugged with an apology, then briskly escorted me out of the wing, down the steps, and through a revolving door that deposited me onto the street.

¤

In Catullus's poem to his dead brother, the otherwise irreverent ancient Roman poet writes (via Anne Carson), "Many the peoples many the oceans I crossed— / . . . so I could give you the last gift owed to death / and talk (why?) with mute ash."

Carson writes of what is otherwise known as "poem 101": "No one (even in Latin) can approximate Catullan diction, which at its most sorrowful has an air of deep festivity, like one of those trees that turns all its leaves over, silver, in the wind . . . I never arrived at the translation I would have liked to do of poem 101. But over the years of working at it, I came to think of translating as a room, not exactly an unknown room, where one gropes for the light switch. I guess it never ends."

¤

When I returned to my flat, it was late enough in the day to call my aunt. I finally had space to cry. We wept together over this early death and our love, bearing the pain of that terrible vacuum that was someone, once. Eventually she handed the phone to my mother, who explained there would be a special urn made for my uncle, which my aunt had decided upon that day. He was cremated the night he died, his ashes waiting. To attempt a new topic, we talked about my morning at the Vatican. How Livilla's icy alabaster urn eluded me. "You must go back," she said, "go back and find it." "It may not be findable," I responded. She pressed me to email again, get the specific location. To work the problem away and hunt until the urn was before me. This began to all feel like a maddening metaphor. To be chasing death when it was right at my feet in a far more significant way. But tasks help the grieving, momentarily. I wrote. I waited.

¤

The procession ends away from the city center, at the place of burial. The pallet and body are placed on a pyre—logs and tinder assembled to hold it and burn. A sow is brought forward and killed. A section of the sow's body is charred and set on the goddess Ceres's altar. Another portion is skewered on a spit and set with the corpse on the funeral pyre. The remainder is a funeral feast—a final meal with the deceased. A close family member sets a torch to the pyre. Perfume and objects for the dead to use in the afterlife are thrown on the flames. Once the burning is complete, the fire is doused with wine.

Livilla received none of these funeral rites. She died in exile on an island, of forced starvation. Hence Agrippina's quiet placement of her urn in her great-grandfather Augustus's remarkable mausoleum. No fanfare, no attention—simply honoring the dead.

The ancient method of cremation, as is true today, only broke things down so far. Whole bones and teeth often remained. The ash was shoveled and placed in an urn, with all its varied elements. In Livilla's time, the urns were egg shaped, or similar to houses with storytelling carvings on their sides. They might have been marble, or alabaster. Or, for the poor, likely clay. If carved, a slot at the top allowed for visitors to drop offerings of flowers and libation to the ashes.

¤

I am not patient, generally. Being thousands of miles away from my loved ones while grieving, starved for an assignment of some kind, didn't help. At the time of sending my follow-up email, I had two more days to see the urn before leaving Rome. One day eased by with no response. On the morning of my final day, I began to research, hoping perhaps to find the location and simply buy a ticket and go.

The Vatican Museum website is confusing at best. Each wing has its own page, but the majority of the text is devoted to the pope who acquired the objects within the wing. The actual artifacts, which often number in the hundreds or thousands, are described as a collection in one or two sentences and with two or three images. Dates are vague. Essentially, they are more focused on proffering information about the different popes who gathered the items than the items themselves. So even though I knew the object type, material, and date, this got me almost nowhere when going through the website of the institution that bore it up on a pedestal within its walls.

I turned elsewhere. Perusing a book, I found a random footnote on Livilla's urn, which referenced another book. Then, there: "Braccio Nuovo, inv. 2302." This was the bright thread to pull. Indeed, "Braccio Nuovo" was a portion of the Vatican: "New Wing," "inv." meaning inventory number. This was it, the exact location. I immediately wrote and requested access. I tried to determine whether I could go to the wing myself, staring at the obscure metro-like Vatican map and website and learning nothing.

Some hours later, I received a response to my request. The turnaround was too quick, they said. It was not possible. I asked if the wing was open—if so, I would purchase a ticket and find the object myself, no escort necessary. "The Braccio Nuovo is closed to the public for restorations and we do not know yet when it will be open again."

Nowhere else to go, I went the Roman cemetery that contains many famous dead (Goethe, Shelley)—but it was Keats I wanted to see. Keats who wrote "On Death," which states, "How strange it is that man on earth should roam, / And lead a life of woe, but not forsake / His rugged path." I set myself on the wooden bench across from his headstone, which does not bear his name but rather, per his request: "Here lies one Whose Name was writ in Water." There were small purple-pink flowers, impossible but there, peeking their way out of the clover at its base. Sun dappled around me. Like a scene from an unsophisticated novel, I sat, stared at the poet's grave, and wept. Perhaps just having a body or grave to weep over gave me something that I needed.

I thought of a short poem by Alejandra Pizarnik, entitled "Silences":

> Death always at my side.
> I listen to what it says.
> And only hear myself.

¤

The ashes are gathered, poured into the white or cream-colored urn, and placed in a crypt. The loved ones huddle around the urn set in a notch. As a group, they speak the word "vale." Farewell.

. . .

Years later, I want to finish this book, seal up my obsession that has hung open for too long. I find the Vatican has updated its websites. From my small apartment on the other side of the world, I realize I can finally lay eyes on Livilla's urn. I click the arrow to move through a wing of cool gray marble with bolts of dark. Gorgeous floor mosaics of fish and gods, dramatic statues nestled in stone niches along the walls. At the wing's center, in a kind of open space with a windowed door, domes with circular skylights, is the urn. It's on an enormous pedestal, between stately life-sized peacocks, their tails folded, and gilding nearly entirely flaked off. A bust labeled pivs vi (the pope who acquired these objects in the late 1700s) is just below. The urn seems huge, but it's hard to say if that's true or the effect of the fish-eye lens. It's shaped like an egg balanced on its narrow head, with two large handles on its sides, its top like a royal chess piece. There are no words carved anywhere, no slot I can see. The stone side facing out looks like something grown in a petri dish. Two uneven light shapes touch, larger than a plate, with light and dark bands of color that circle around them. Its back is less dramatic, or differently so. The cracks it has sustained are there, but it is whole. I can't tell if these pieces were reassembled. If the dark between the cracks is the gunk of time or put there with care. *Is she in there?* I wonder. Rings and rings of light color, the palest, grayest pink. I zoom in closer than I would be allowed to lean if I were in the room. I want to press a hand on the cool stone. Run a nail along the rings. Wonder if Agrippina did this, but perhaps she had no possibility or interest in such drama. I suppose this is the best I can do.

NOTES

Some quotations of ancient texts were slightly revised for readability.

Epigraphs

vii **"History is a kind of study."** Solmaz Sharif, *Customs* (Graywolf, 2022).

vii **"I am not inventing marvels . . .":** Tacitus, *The Annals of Imperial Rome*, trans. Michael Grant (Penguin, 1973).

"Agrippina the Younger"

3 **Agrippina the Younger:** fourth child of Agrippina the Elder and Germanicus, empress of Rome, sister of Emperor Caligula, wife of Emperor Claudius, mother of Emperor Nero. Very little is known about the life of Agrippina the Younger. Agrippina's three memoirs included two casus suorii (the misfortunes of a mother's or father's family) and a de vita eius (a chronology of one's own life). Many Roman rulers penned a de vita sua, mostly chronicling their military and political successes. None of Agrippina's memoirs have survived. In Pliny the Elder's *Natural History* he cites Agrippina's writing under "Of Prodigious and Monstrous Births," as she apparently described Nero's breech birth in her text. The fact she recounted her experience giving birth in a piece of writing otherwise used to describe martial and political gains gives us some insight into Agrippina's character.

3 **Nero:** son of Agrippina the Younger and Domitius. Nero became emperor at sixteen years of age, and his reign ended in suicide at age thirty after fleeing Rome. While Nero is often likened to Caligula, in many ways he was a worse leader than his infamous uncle—if only for his total lack of political experience prior to becoming emperor. Nero exploited his power for personal gain and, after some years, focused more on music and performance than his political responsibilities.

3 **Piso:** savvy politician who served Emperors Augustus and Tiberius. He and Germanicus had several tussles over power, perhaps at the goading of Tiberius. After becoming ill, Germanicus was convinced Piso had

poisoned him. There was a trial, during which Piso died by suicide or, some believe, was assassinated on Tiberius's order. While Piso was not found guilty of murdering Germanicus, he was convicted of far lesser crimes and was given the sentence of damnatio memoriae—in essence, to be removed from the historical record. The damnatio memoriae was the most terrible sentence a Roman could receive.

▽

7 **"What can History possibly say?"**: Robin Coste Lewis, *Voyage of the Sable Venus and Other Poems* (Knopf, 2015).

"Agrippina Becomes the First Noblewoman to Give Birth on Campaign . . ."

9 **Oppidum Ubiorum:** renamed Colonia Claudia Ara Agrippinensium in honor of Agrippina the Younger. Modern-day Cologne, Germany.

9 **Agrippina the Elder:** wife of Germanicus, mother of Agrippina the Younger and Emperor Caligula. She was generally beloved, despite in many ways being an iconoclast. Her fertility, along with her lineage and her devotion to Germanicus, were great assets in the eyes of Romans. She impacted her husband's political decisions and had serious ambitions for her six children. Agrippina the Elder was the first woman of her stature to go on campaign with her husband. She was also remarkably brave, once quelling a mutiny over burning a bridge over the Rhine to halt the passage of the enemy. Not long after the soldiers calmed down, lost allies arrived and made their way over the bridge to safety.

"Germanicus's Recovering Two of Three Golden Eagle Standards"

12 **Germanicus:** husband of Agrippina the Elder, adopted son of Emperor Tiberius, father of Agrippina the Younger and Emperor Caligula, famous Roman general. Germanicus was roundly loved and considered to embody the ideal Roman. He was an excellent soldier, general, and politician. He came from a noble family and married a woman descended from Caesar, Agrippina the Elder, with whom he had many children. Prior to his death, he was heir apparent to the Roman imperial seat.

12 **aquila:** eagle standard. Each Roman legion carried with it a numbered standard bearing the image of a golden eagle. The Romans invested remarkable significance in the aquilae—if one was lost, the military expended immense efforts to recover it. Six years after the Battle of the Teutoburg Forest, during which three Roman legions were destroyed and their respective aquilae taken, Germanicus successfully recovered two of them, vaulting him even further into fame.

12 **Tiberius:** son of Empress Livia and adopted son of Emperor Augustus. While an excellent general, Tiberius was not a great emperor. He was generally cruel, solitary, and paranoid. He eventually went to the isolated island of Capri, depending on a praetorian prefect, Sejanus, to handle logistics back in Rome. There is much speculation that Caligula played a role in Emperor Tiberius's death.

"The Tiber"

14 "as many as twenty being so treated in a single day . . ."; "mud kneaded with blood . . ."; "those who wished to die . . ."; "had the power of seeing . . .": Suetonius, *The Lives of the Twelve Caesars*, trans. C. Rolfe (Harvard University Press, 1914).

14 **Suetonius:** Roman historian and author of *The Lives of the Twelve Caesars* (*De vita Caesarum*). This text chronicles the lives of Rome's leaders from Julius Caesar to Domitian. Along with their narratives, Suetonius includes many tidbits including quotations from the rulers, their habits, family lines, and appearance—as well as omens and rumors.

14 "The sources need to be seen as texts that have a clear agenda . . .": Thorsten Opper quoted in Livia Gershon, "Was Emperor Nero Really as Monstrous as History Suggests?" *Smithsonian Magazine*, May 25, 2021.

"The Mausoleum of Augustus"

19 "a city-block-sized monument . . .": Tom Kington, "Emperor Augustus Stables in Rome to Be Reburied due to Lack of Funding," *The Telegraph*, August 17, 2014, https://www.telegraph.co.uk/news/worldnews /europe/italy/11039874/Emperor-Augustus-stables-in-Rome-to-be -reburied-due-to-lack-of-funding.html.

"The Death of Germanicus and the Early Message of Its Approach"

20 **Oracle of Apollo at Claros:** oracle situated in a temple of the god Apollo, located on the Ionian coast of the Mediterranean Sea near Colophon (in modern-day İzmir Province, Turkey). This oracle was once as famous a source for prophesy as the oracle of Apollo at Delphi. Oracles of classical antiquity were believed to essentially channel a specific god, in this case Apollo, directly to the public. Oracles, as conduits for godly transmissions, gave infallible prophesies. Any potential inaccuracies were chalked up to people misinterpreting the real intention of what the oracle said (which was generally ambiguous).

21 **"some flung their household gods into the street . . .":** Suetonius, *The Lives of the Twelve Caesars*, trans. Rolfe.

"The Mausoleum of Augustus"

22 **Augustus:** first emperor of Rome, husband of Empress Livia, and adoptive father of Emperor Tiberius. Only eighteen when his granduncle Julius Caesar was assassinated, putting him on the throne, Augustus was the first and arguably the most successful ruler of the empire. Augustus was an extremely savvy politician and military leader, and his reforms and developments in city infrastructure, military, government, and imperial expansion were remarkable. He arguably defined the role of Roman emperor.

22 **"Janus Quirinus, which our ancestors ordered . . .":** Paterculus, Velleius, and Augustus, *Compendium of Roman History*, trans. Frederick W. Shipley (Harvard University Press, 1924).

22 **"He was so far from being particular . . .":** Suetonius, *The Lives of the Twelve Caesars*, trans. Rolfe.

"The Lupercal"

25 **Romulus and Remus:** twin brothers whose apocryphal origin story is tied to the founding of Rome. The twin brothers, thought to be a threat to the king, were abandoned on the edge of the Tiber River. Instead of dying, the twins were taken to a cave and suckled by a she-wolf in

what was later called the Lupercal. As young men, they set out to start a great city of their own but quarreled over which hill (Rome has seven) to build upon. Ultimately, Romulus killed Remus over this dispute, became king, and founded the city of Rome.

25 **"Could it be that a local whore..."**: Mary Beard, *SPQR: A History of Ancient Rome* (Liveright, 2015).

25 **"a bitter fate pursues the Romans..."**: Horace, *Odes and Epodes*, trans. C. E. Bennett (Harvard University Press, 1914).

"The House of Livia"

27 **Livia:** first empress of Rome, wife of Emperor Augustus, mother of Emperor Tiberius. Extremely powerful and known for her ability to influence her husband, Livia is a kind of proto-Agrippina. She worked hard to get her son Tiberius the imperial seat and for a time had an impact on his rule. Her recognition that a male child is a means for power likely impacted Agrippina the Younger's behavior, too. Livia paved the way for future empresses to have more agency. With imperial Rome, the empress had the ability to impress upon her husband her ideas regarding whatever concerned her and potentially have a real impact on his rule. This, many senators and magistrates believed, was a terrible side effect of the government as it transitioned from a republic into an empire. Livia also transformed the often-sequestered role of "ideal" matriarch, largely defined by modesty and domestic responsibilities, into a public-facing one.

27 **"Because I was a woman..."**: *I, Claudius*, episode 4, "Poison Is Queen," directed by Herbert Wise, featuring Siân Phillips, aired October 11, 1976, on BBC Television. The series is based on a novel by Robert Graves.

"Agrippina After Her Mother Tells Her Emperor Tiberius Is Giving Her Over to Marriage"

28 **Domitius:** first husband of Agrippina the Younger, father of Emperor Nero. Domitius was largely considered heartless, duplicitous, and violent.

28 **Praetor:** commander of a Roman army or an elected magistrate.

"The House of Livia"

32 **"loved and esteemed her . . ."; "she took an egg . . ."**: Suetonius, *The Lives of the Twelve Caesars*, trans. Rolfe.

"The Island of Capri"

35 **Caligula:** third child of Agrippina the Elder and Germanicus, emperor of Rome. Born Gaius, he was given the name "Little Boots" (a diminutive form of caligae) by soldiers for the soldier's outfit he wore while on campaign with his father in Germania. (Apparently no one called him by this name in adulthood, but, strangely, it has stuck.) Caligula was an undeniably good emperor at the beginning of his four-year reign. By his death he had become the most famously cruel, insane, and damaging emperor yet. There are many theories regarding his transformation, most involving a bout of illness in 37 C.E. There is a possibility he suffered from epilepsy, hyperthyroidism, meningitis, or encephalitis—or was simply poisoned. He was the first Roman emperor to be assassinated (Julius Caesar had the title of dictator, not emperor).

35 **"unweaned babies put to his . . ."; "cast headlong into the sea . . ."; "rearing a viper for the Roman people"**: Suetonius, *The Lives of the Twelve Caesars*, trans. Rolfe.

36 **"anomalous creatures have long been displayed . . ."**: Leslie Fielder, *The Tyranny of the Normal: Essays on Bioethics, Theology and Myth* (David R. Godine, 1996).

"The Exile of Agrippina's Mother by the Emperor Tiberius for Four Years . . ."

37 **"one tells his guard . . ."**: first child of Agrippina the Elder and Germanicus, uncle of Emperor Nero. After the deaths of the two men meant to inherit the role of emperor (Germanicus and then Emperor Tiberius's son), Tiberius adopted Drusus and his brother Nero (Agrippina the Younger's brother—*not* her son) in order to secure their joint rule after Tiberius's death. Yet Tiberius ultimately decided against having his adopted grandsons as heirs. Due to accusations from Emperor Tiberius, the Senate exiled Nero to the island of Pontia, where he was later assassinated or compelled to die by suicide. Once made emperor six years

later, Caligula placed his brother Nero's remains in the Mausoleum of Augustus.

37 **"The other swallows pinched bed . . .":** second child of Agrippina the Elder and Germanicus. Like his brother Nero, Drusus was the adopted grandson of Emperor Tiberius. Tiberius eventually had a change of heart and exiled Drusus, who starved to death after three years's imprisonment. Drusus tried to stave off death by eating his bed stuffing.

"Agrippina's Birth of Her Son, / Future Emperor Nero"

40 **"Pliny writes . . .":** "Agrippina, too, the mother of Nero, who was lately Emperor, and who proved himself, throughout the whole of his reign, the enemy of the human race, has left it recorded in writing, that he was born with his feet first." Pliny the Elder, *The Natural History of Pliny*, trans. John Bostock and Henry Thomas Riley (George Bell & Sons, 1890).

▽

41 **"if a woman fights . . .":** Hilda Doolittle, *Helen in Egypt* (New Directions, 1961).

"My Theory for Caligula's Change"

45 **Drusilla:** fifth child of Agrippina the Elder and Germanicus. Generally regarded as the favorite of Caligula, Drusilla was the only of her six siblings to die a natural death. When Emperor Caligula was ill, he named her his heir. She was the first Roman woman to receive the honor.

"If Caligula Had Incestuous Desire . . ."

46 **Livilla:** sixth and youngest child of Agrippina the Elder and Germanicus. Livilla was exiled, by some accounts, with her sister Agrippina the Younger to Pandateria—or to Tyrrhenia. Or they were separated. She was later exiled to the same island again (or perhaps the other!), under the assertion she was having an affair with Seneca (who was also subsequently exiled). Livilla's urn is the only one that survives from the Mausoleum of Augustus.

"Caligula's Changing"

51 **the actor from *A Clockwork Orange*:** Malcolm McDowell in *Caligula*.

51 **the other actor from *Alien*:** John Hurt in *I, Claudius*.

52 **"had no more chance . . .":** Suetonius, *The Lives of the Twelve Caesars*, trans. Rolfe.

"Caligula Starts with the Forced Suicide of His Adopted Son . . ."

53 **Claudius:** fourth emperor of Rome, uncle and husband to Agrippina the Younger. Claudius had a stutter and a limp, for which his family apparently made fun of him of throughout his life. He was never considered a threat to power, so Caligula never ordered his death. Claudius ended up succeeding his nephew, marrying his own niece Agrippina the Younger, and adopting her son Nero. He is largely known for his pliancy under his wives and advisers.

53 **"Drusilla's widower . . ."** Lepidus, husband of Drusilla and possible lover of Caligula. At one point Lepidus was Caligula's heir, prior to Lepidus's (possibly falsified) conspiracy with Agrippina and Livilla against Caligula and Lepidus's subsequent execution. Per Senate order, Lepidus was denied a proper burial.

"The Island of Pandateria, Now Ventotene"

55 **"Each Cell is an island . . .":** Jeremy Bentham, *The Works of Jeremy Bentham* (William Tait, 1838–43).

"The Assassination of Emperor Caligula"

56 **Praetorian Guard:** elite soldiers who served as bodyguards to the emperor.

"The Cryptoporticus—Palatine Hill"

57 **Consuls:** the most powerful figures in preimperial Rome. With the rise of the empire in 27 C.E., consuls continued to have honorary status, but power was consolidated into the hands of the emperor.

57 **"Strike so that he . . ."; "What do you suppose . . .":** Suetonius, *The Lives of the Twelve Caesars*, trans. Rolfe.

57 **Julius Caesar:** Roman dictator whose assassination ultimately ended the Roman Republic. After Caesar's death, a series of civil wars transformed Rome from a republic (with the Senate as the most powerful branch of government) to an empire (with an emperor in the highest seat of power). Caesar had named his grandnephew Gaius Octavius (later Augustus) his heir after a shuffling of power, Augustus ultimately became the first emperor of the Roman Empire. Caesar was the first Roman to be deified, allowing Augustus to call himself DIVI FILIUS, son of a god.

"Passienus"

58 **Passienus:** twice consul, second husband of Agrippina the Younger, stepfather to future Emperor Nero, ex-husband of Domitia. Passienus divorced Domitia, who was a sister-in-law and enemy of Agrippina, and married Agrippina. For Agrippina to marry a wonderful person after her marriage to the cruel Domitius—and to also have the joy of revenge against her sister-in-law Domitia—feels like poetic justice.

58 **Domitia:** sister of Domitius, aunt of Emperor Nero, ex-wife of Passienus. Domitia is shorthand for Domitia Lepida the Elder (as her sister had the same name but was "the Younger"). She hated Agrippina the Younger, her sister-in-law. Domitia watched over Nero while Agrippina was in exile and after Domitius's death.

"When Empress Messalina Potentially Decides the Son of Agrippina . . ."

59 **Messalina:** empress and third wife of Emperor Claudius, mother of Britannicus and Octavia. For many ancient Roman historians, Messalina was a strange counterpoint to Agrippina the Younger. Where Agrippina wanted power, Messalina wanted sexual pleasure. Deviant sexual desire was a frequently used smear tactic, however, and in all likelihood this representation is inaccurate.

59 **Britannicus:** son of Emperor Claudius and Empress Messalina. Initially Claudius's young heir, Britannicus was born not long after Claudius assumed the imperial seat. Following the downfall and death of Messalina, Claudius married Agrippina the Younger, and Agrippina's son Nero became a competitor for heir to the throne. Following the death of Claudius in 54 C.E., Nero claimed power. Britannicus remained a threat, however, and within the year he was dead, likely poisoned by Emperor Nero.

"The Attempted Assassination of Agrippina's Son During Sleep"

61 "and afterwards...": Suetonius, *The Lives of the Twelve Caesars*, trans. Rolfe.

"The Vatican Museum"

62 "so infected it as to kill the fish...": Suetonius, *The Lives of the Twelve Caesars*, trans. Rolfe.

62 "The victor's perspective is so dominating...": Beard, *SPQR*.

"Agrippina the Younger's Marriage to Emperor Claudius..."

64 "perhaps wanted another politician...": Silius, Roman senator. Some accounts claim that Silius plotted with Empress Messalina so that he might adopt Britannicus and become emperor until the boy came of age, and that to this end Silius and Messalina married in public while Claudius was away. It is more likely that, while they were lovers, the two simply had a party for Bacchus. Claudius's advisers, hating Messalina, took the festivities as an opportunity to convince the emperor that his wife was a traitor. In any case, Claudius returned and ordered many quick trials and executions. Silius died by suicide the night Claudius returned to Rome.

64 **Narcissus:** freedman who served as secretary to Emperor Claudius. The emperor's right-hand man, it was Narcissus who warned Claudius of the empress's "marriage," which may have been part of a plot to overthrow him. Narcissus's loyalty was so great that, following Claudius's

death and knowing that he himself would be executed, Narcissus still returned to Rome so he could burn all of Claudius's letters to avoid them falling into the wrong hands. Apparently, Narcissus had a little white dog that followed him around, a detail I love.

"The Celtic Chieftain Caratacus Captured..."

68 **Caratacus:** Celtic chieftain renowned for leading the resistance against the Roman invasion. After his capture, Caratacus famously gave a speech appealing to Emperor Claudius to spare his life—which Claudius did.

▽

69 "If you'd been born...": Trisha Low, *Socialist Realism* (Coffee House Press, 2019).

"The Augustan Sanctuary and Residential Complex"

71 "covering the remains of Augustus's marbled...": Kington, "Emperor Augustus Stables in Rome to Be Reburied due to Lack of Funding."

72 "As soon as he began...": Suetonius, *The Lives of the Twelve Caesars*, trans. Rolfe.

72 "blueprint that every emperor for..."; "one of the saddest losses...": Beard, *SPQR*.

"Future Emperor Nero Assumes the Toga Virilis..."

73 **toga virilis:** literally "man's robe," a toga that denotes that its wearer has graduated to adult male citizenship.

"The Colosseum"

74 "pointedly built on the site...": Beard, *SPQR*.

"The Death of Emperor Claudius at Age Sixty-Three..."

75 **Locusta:** a poison expert under Empress Agrippina the Younger, then Emperor Nero. Locusta apparently trained others in her craft of poisoning on her estate, which Nero gave to her after Britannicus's death. Once Galba became emperor, he had Locusta executed.

"The Brief Period of Agrippina Holding Total Power Through Her Emperor-Son"

76 **Seneca:** philosopher, statesman, Emperor Nero's closest adviser. Seneca had many accomplishments beyond his philosophy. While a senator, Seneca was known for his expertise as an orator—his talent so annoyed Emperor Caligula he ordered Seneca to suicide. Seneca survived only because he was ill at the time and Caligula was convinced he would die soon anyway (the senator recovered). Seneca was sent to exile on Corsica during Emperor Claudius's reign, ostensibly for having an affair with Livilla (sister to Agrippina the Younger). Once Agrippina became empress, she recalled Seneca to serve as Nero's tutor. After Nero became emperor, Seneca worked closely with Burrus to serve as adviser to Nero. Seneca apparently wrote many of Nero's speeches and had an enormous influence on his decisions. As Nero became more despotic, Seneca tried to retire multiple times. Nero denied permission, so Seneca spent most of the time out of the city. Nero eventually thought Seneca had a role in a conspiracy and ordered him to suicide.

76 **Burrus:** adviser to Emperor Nero, prefect of the Praetorian Guard. Agrippina the Younger appointed Burrus prefect after Claudius's death. Burrus worked with Seneca to advise Nero during his reign, ultimately betraying Agrippina. Nero eventually turned on Burrus, too.

"The Island of Capri"

77 "The mute freak is a . . .": Rosemarie Garland Thompson, *Extraordinary Bodies: Figuring Physical Disability in American Culture and Literature* (Columbia University Press, 1997).

77 "animal within the animal . . .": Aretaeus of Cappadocia, *The Extant Works of Aretaeus the Cappadocian*, trans. Francis Adams (Printed for the Sydenham Society, 1856).

"Emperor Nero After the Assassination of His Mother, Agrippina"

84 "Let him kill me as . . .": Cornelius Tacitus, *The Annals of Imperial Rome*, trans. J. Jackson (Harvard University Press, 1925).

84 "was hounded by his mother's...": Suetonius, *The Lives of the Twelve Caesars*, trans. Rolfe.

"The Bay of Baiae"

86 "Possibly as a final touch of hypocrisy..."; "a woman gave birth to a serpent...": Tacitus, *Annals of Imperial Rome*, trans. Jackson.

86 "one long, epic movie...": *Quo Vadis* (dir. Mervyn LeRoy and Anthony Mann, 1951) with Peter Ustinov as Nero.

86 "She plotted to be the mother to the whole world...": Mutsuo Takahashi, *Only Yesterday*, trans. Jeffrey Angles (Canarium, 2023).

86 **Tacitus:** ancient Roman historian and senator. Born a little over a decade before Nero's death, Tacitus wrote the *Annals*, which is generally revered for its descriptions of the events surrounding Emperors Tiberius, Caligula, Claudius, and Nero. Apparently, as a senator, Tacitus had access to Senate records, upon which he based his historical writing.

"The Uprising of Over 200,000 Tribespeople..."

87 **Boudica:** queen of a Celtic a tribe who famously led an uprising against Roman occupiers. After the Romans denied her power bequeathed to her and her daughters by her late husband King Prasutagus, Queen Boudica rallied tens of thousands of local tribespeople in an uprising across Britain. They moved through several Roman cities and settlements (including modern London), killing and torturing one hundred thousand enemies and burning all they could. They took no prisoners. There are different versions of Boudica's death, including simply illness. Though Boudica's forces ultimately failed, she is an enduring icon in British (and particularly Welsh) culture. There is a large brass statue entitled *Boadicea and Her Daughters* on the Victoria Embankment in London, a city Boudica and her compatriots destroyed.

88 "as a sign that no war...": Suetonius, *The Lives of the Twelve Caesars*, trans. Rolfe.

"Nero's Domus Aurea"

90 "at last beginning to be . . ."; "There was nothing however in . . .": Suetonius, *The Lives of the Twelve Caesars*, trans. Rolfe.

91 "**He was a spoiled young aristocrat . . .**": Thorsten Opper quoted in Rebecca Mead, "How Nasty Was Nero, Really?" *The New Yorker*, June 7, 2021, https://www.newyorker.com/magazine/2021/06/14/how-nasty-was-nero-really.

91 "**Seneca wrote the play around . . .**": Mead, "How Nasty Was Nero, Really?"

"The Death of Emperor Nero"

92 **Octavia:** daughter of Emperor Claudius and Empress Messalina, wife of Emperor Nero. Nero abused Octavia emotionally, physically, and politically. She attended the dinner where Nero had her younger brother Britannicus poisoned. After he impregnated his mistress, a freedwoman named Poppaea, Nero divorced Octavia, claiming she was barren. Octavia died at the age of twenty-two by Emperor Nero's order, in exile on the same island where Agrippina the Elder and Livilla died.

92 **Tribune:** title for a variety of elected officials.

92 **Centurion:** high-ranking officer in the Roman army.

92 **Sporus:** spouse of Emperor Nero at the time of the emperor's death. This relationship occurred following the death of Poppaea, the second wife of Emperor Nero, after Nero kicked her in the gut while she was pregnant (she likely died in childbirth). Following Poppaea's death, Nero found a young boy, Sporus, who looked uncannily similar to his wife. Nero had Sporus castrated and then married him, with Sporus wearing an empress's regalia. Indeed, Sporus was often addressed as "mistress" or "empress." Sporus died by suicide at around twenty years old.

"The Mausoleum of Augustus"

94 "**My voice sticks . . .**": Saint Jerome, *A Select Library of Nicene and Post-Nicene Fathers of the Christian Church: St. Jerome Letters and Selected Works*, trans. Philip Schaff and Henry Wace (Parker, 1893).

"Elsewhere"

95 **"The meek shall inherit..."**: dictum attributed to John Paul Getty.

95 **"Ask yourself whenever you're looking..."**: "Mary Beard's Favourite Objects from *Nero: The Man Behind the Myth*," August 26, 2021, British Museum, YouTube, https://youtu.be/Hywug2mmoQc.

"Addendum—Livilla's Urn"

96 **"It is a dangerous myth..."**: Beard, *SPQR*.

100 **"Many the peoples..."; "No one (even in Latin)..."**: Anne Carson, *NOX* (New Directions, 2010).

103 **"Death always at my side..."**: Alejandra Pizarnik, "Silences," in *Extracting the Stone of Madness*, trans. Yvette Siegert (New Directions, 2000).

ACKNOWLEDGMENTS

The following journals published or featured (often earlier versions) of these pieces. Many thanks to their editors and staff for their support of my work and the larger literary community.

Action, Spectacle—"Germanicus's Recovering . . ."

BOMB—"The Rhine," "Agrippina, Age Five"

Black Warrior Review—"Agrippina the Younger"

Columbia Journal—"Caligula's Changing"

The Georgia Review—"The Death of Germanicus . . ." "Agrippina After Her Mother Tells Her . . ." "Future Emperor Nero Assumes the Toga Virilis . . ." "The Great Fire of Rome"

Harvard Review—"The Cryptoporticus—Palatine Hill"

Los Angeles Review of Books—"Livilla's Urn"

PoetryNow and the Poetry Foundation website—"Agrippina, Age Thirteen"

Salt Hill—"Agrippina, Age Three"

¤

Creating takes a village. Dozens of people, known and unknown to me, provided support so that I might write these poems. This book wouldn't be possible without them. I extend my deep thanks to:

SUSAN MCCABE AND HER POETRY WORKSHOP for suggesting I write beyond that first poem about Agrippina.

ALICE NOTLEY for telling me to write a book about Agrippina after seeing a sheaf of early poems.

SARAH VAP for going through this so closely.

CARMEN GIMÉNEZ for pushing me to look differently.

IN ADDITION, THOSE WHO READ AND PRODDED: Mary-Kim Arnold, Todd Fredson, Sarah Gzemski, Amy Lawless, Robin Coste Lewis, Ruth Madievsky, Douglas Manuel, Anna Moschovakis, Vi Khi Nao, Brandon Som, David St. John, and Ben White.

THE INSTITUTIONS AND STAFF THAT PROVIDED ME TIME, FUNDING, AND SUPPORT: Caldera Artist's Residency, Yaddo Artist's Residency, University of Southern California Center for Feminist Research, and the Vatican Museums.

THE NORTHWESTERN UNIVERSITY PRESS/CURBSTONE TEAM for their belief in this book and shepherding it out into the world. Everyone was so wonderful and helpful: Marisa Seigel (this book's acquisitions editor), Maia Rigas (this book's editor), Kristen Twardowski (sales and marketing), Maddie Schultz (marketing coordinator), Charlotte Keathley (publicity), Courtney Smotherman (rights and permissions). Many thanks, too, to those behind the scenes at Northwestern not listed here who helped make the book possible. I was choosy with finding this book a home—I'm thoroughly honored. In addition, my wonderful publicist Alisha Gorder (from Pine State Publicity).

MY FAMILY AND FRIENDS, AND ALI AND OUR CATS HOMER AND SAPPHO (may she continue to bite pencils in the heavens). You all helped me in vital ways as I wrestled in the muck with this work.

AND MY MOTHER, who fought for agency for herself and vulnerable people her whole life. Vale—goodbye, and hello, always.

CREDITS

Solmaz Sharif, excerpt from "Social Skills Training" from *Customs: Poems*. Copyright © 2022 by Solmaz Sharif. Reprinted with the permission of The Permissions Company, LLC, on behalf of Graywolf Press, graywolfpress.org, and Bloomsbury Poetry, an imprint of Bloomsbury Publishing PLC.

Tacitus, *The Annals of Imperial Rome*, Penguin Classics. Copyright © Michael Grant Publications Ltd, 1956, 1959, 1971, 1973, 1975, 1977, 1989, 1996. Reprinted by permission of Penguin Books Limited.

Family tree drawn by Dylan Farr, https://www.dylanfarranimation.com.

"Félicité," from *Voyage of The Sable Venus: And Other Poems* by Robin Coste Lewis, copyright © 2015 by Robin Coste Lewis. Used by permission of Alfred A. Knopf, an imprint of the Knopf Doubleday Publishing Group, a division of Penguin Random House LLC. All rights reserved.

Leslie Fiedler, excerpt from the introduction to *The Tyranny of the Normal: Essays on Bioethics, Theology, and Myth*. Copyright © 1996 by Leslie Fiedler. Reprinted with the permission of The Permissions Company, LLC on behalf of David R. Godine, Publisher, Inc., www.godine.com.

Excerpt by Hilda Doolittle, from *Helen in Egypt*, copyright © 1961 by Norman Holmes Pearson. Reprinted by permission of New Directions Publishing Corp and Carcanet Press.

Excerpt is used by permission from Trisha Low, *Socialist Realism* (Coffee House Press, 2019). Copyright © 2019 by Trisha Low.

Excerpt from Rosemarie Garland Thomson, *Extraordinary Bodies: Figuring Physical Disability in American Culture and Literature*. Copyright © 1997 Rosemarie Garland Thomson. Reprinted with permission of Columbia University Press.

Rebecca Mead, excerpt from "How Nasty Was Nero, Really?" *The New Yorker*, June 7, 2021. Copyright © 2021 by Rebecca Mead. Reprinted with the permission of the author.

"Catullus 101" (brief excerpt) by Anne Carson, from *NOX*, copyright © 2010 by Anne Carson. Reprinted by permission of New Directions Publishing Corp.

"Silences," by Alejandra Pizarnik, translated by Yvette Siegert, from *Extracting the Stone of Madness: Poems, 1962–1972*, copyright © 2000 by Miriam Pizarnik. Translation copyright © 2016 by Yvette Siegert. Reprinted by permission of New Directions Publishing Corp.